Women's Figures

THE ECONOMIC PROGRESS OF WOMEN IN AMERICA

Diana Furchtgott-Roth
American Enterprise
Institute
&
Christine Stolba
Emory University

Women's Figures (ISBN: 0-8447-7083-3) is a publication of the Independent Women's Forum, a nonprofit, nonpartisan organization established in 1992. Through its activities, IWF promotes public education and debate, and provides a voice for women and men who believe in freedom, opportunity, and individual responsibility.

In addition to *Women's Figures*, IWF publishes *The Women's Quarterly*, a periodical featuring lively, informative articles by and about women, and the IWF newsletter, *Ex Femina*. IWF also produces the *Media Directory of Women Experts* (1995), now available on-line at IWF's website http:/**www.iwf.org.**

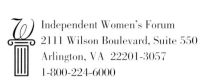 Independent Women's Forum
2111 Wilson Boulevard, Suite 550
Arlington, VA 22201-3057
1-800-224-6000

Art and design by Mitzi Hamilton for Bird-in-Hand Productions, Toronto.
Graphs by Norman Chaykoski, Toronto.
Special thanks to Nina Santos, CLB Printing Co., Kensington, Md.

Table of Contents

ACKNOWLEDGMENTS

Women's Figures reflects the efforts of many individuals.

Leah Seppanen of AEI patiently and conscientiously constructed the graphs, collected and updated each data series, reconciled inconsistencies in the text, and provided editorial suggestions. Audrey Williams of AEI did a superb job of updating the drafts, keeping track of different versions of the manuscript, and incorporating numerous changes. AEI interns Tiger Craft, Chelsea Haga, Katherine Harness, and Jennifer Wagner searched for data both on the internet and in libraries and constructed graphs. This monograph would not have been completed without them.

Special thanks go to those who took the time to read and comment on early versions of the work, including Karlyn Bowman, Marvin Kosters, and Leigh Tripoli of AEI, Arlene Holen of the U.S. Congressional Budget Office, Amy Holmes of the Independent Women's Forum, and Wendy Lee Gramm, former chairman of the Commodity Futures Trading Commission and board member of the Independent Women's Forum. Their insightful comments vastly improved both the structure and the message. Only the errors are the authors' own work.

The authors would also like to thank Christopher DeMuth, AEI president, and David Gerson, AEI executive vice president, who showed a great interest in the topic and made resources available for the project's completion.

This project would not have been started without Barbara Ledeen and Anita Blair of the Independent Women's Forum. Their support and encouragement are much appreciated.

Ms. Furchtgott-Roth is a resident fellow and assistant to the president at the American Enterprise Institute, Washington, D.C.

Ms. Stolba is a Ph.D. candidate in American History at Emory University, Atlanta, Georgia.

Foreword

A major thesis of popular media culture is that women are victims of their social condition. According to that theory, women suffer from substantial discrimination that leaves them less well-off than men. The apostles of that women-as-victims perspective use selected statistics and anecdotes to illustrate their theory. For example, women are depicted as earning consistently less than men. The corollary to that theory is that only government intervention can eradicate this discrimination to achieve parity between men and women.

Women's Figures is a brief interpretation of historical data comparing women and men in America. Those data are woven together with explanations of the empirical evidence. The monograph shows how women's wages and education levels are closing the gap with those of men; how occupational choices have influenced wages; and how women are playing an important role in creating small businesses.

The evidence on the status of women in society is far more complex than the women-as-victims theory can explain. Women have made substantial progress in labor markets as a result of changes in technology, social attitudes, and laws. In many cases where women remain behind men, market forces explain outcomes more readily than overt discrimination. Even where there may be discrimination, there is little if any evidence that expanded government intervention would serve any useful purpose.

Wage Gap

98¢: The disappearing wage gap...

■ *National Longitudinal Survey of Youth* data show that among people ages 27 to 33 who have never had a child, **women's earnings approach 98 percent of men's earnings.**

■ Women's success over time—the Department of Labor reports that from 1920 to 1980, women's wages grew at a rate 20 percent faster than men's wages.

■ According to economist June O'Neill, "When earnings comparisons are restricted to men and women more similar in their experience and life situations, the **measured earnings differentials are typically quite small.**"

■ Women in college and university administration, engineering, and economics, for example, earn as much as (and sometimes more than) men in the same fields.

Women are quickly closing in

Women will continue to enter previously male-dominated, higher paying fields like engineering, and, accounting for job characteristics, the already negligible differences will disappear.

Q & A

What about the other two cents?

The two-cent difference might be accounted for by discrimination not yet eliminated, by differences between men and women that are unaccounted for, or by other factors not included in the studies.

Why do most figures on the wage gap claim a larger wage difference, usually about seventy-two cents for every male dollar?

Most comparisons fail to take into account underlying factors such as educational attainment, field of employment, work experience, and women's personal choices.

Glass
Ceiling

Shattering the glass ceiling myth

■ A recent Korn/Ferry Study of the achievement of corporate executives in the past decade found that the **number of female executive vice-presidents more than doubled** and the **number of female senior vice-presidents increased by 75 percent.**

■ The *Glass Ceiling Commission Report* compared the number of women in the total labor force (without reference to experience or education levels) with the number wielding power in *Fortune* 2000 companies. A more accurate study would have compared women in the qualified labor pool (which for senior management positions is typically an MBA and twenty-five years of work experience) with the number of women who have actually achieved such senior positions.

■ Statistics tend to support the "pipeline theory" of women's corporate advancement. Labor force participation rates reveal that women have been working in significant numbers for about only thirty years.

■ The *Glass Ceiling Commission Report* examined only *Fortune*

2000 companies, which represent only a small portion of the economy. Given evidence of women's impressive gains in starting their own businesses, for example, this report says little about women's success in the American economy as a whole.

■ "Even if sexism disappeared from corporate boardrooms tomorrow, the *Fortune* 500 might never see 250 chief executives in skirts. Two-thirds of all graduates in business and similar subjects are still men. Men rarely have to balance the demands of work and family, as women often do."—"Through a Glass, Darkly," *Economist*, August 19, 1996

Pipeline to the future

As women continue to go "through the pipeline," steadily increasing their numbers in previously male-dominated educational fields and professions, more women will achieve top senior management positions in business and other fields.

Q & A

Why should we have to wait for women to become CEOs on a par with men? Why can't women reach the top now?

Turn the question around. Is it reasonable to expect that a woman with only seven consecutive years of work experience (a woman who might have, for example, taken time away from work to raise a family) would surpass another woman or a man who has been working for fourteen consecutive years? In the executive suite, as in the general job market, experience pays.

Pink Ghetto

What a mom needs most: options

■ "Sixty-three percent of mothers with children age five and under gave high priority to getting paid leave to care for children."—recent U.S. Department of Labor report, *Working Women Count*, "Executive Summary"

■ "Even highly successful women frequently want to spend much more time with their young children than the sixty-hour weeks required by the corporate fast track will permit."—Elizabeth Fox-Genovese

■ Many women choose to enter the "pink ghetto" because the jobs offer much-needed flexibility; job skills are also more likely to deteriorate slowly in these fields, allowing women to leave the workforce for a time—to have children for example—and still retain the skills needed to be viable job candidates when they return.

■ "Although pay in women's occupations has been found to be

lower than pay in typically male occupations, this fact alone is not evidence of employer discrimination." —Economist June O'Neill

■ A 1995 study by Claudia Goldin, a research associate at the National Bureau of Economic Research, found that only about 15 percent of women questioned who received college degrees around 1972 were maintaining both career and family. Among those who have had a successful career, as indicated by income level, nearly 50 percent were childless. More recent graduates are increasingly combining career and family.

Flexing our options

More companies will find that flexibility enhances their work-force capability. Both men and women benefit from flex-time.

Q & A:

It seems to me that even if women are getting equal pay for equal work, the fact is that we're not getting equal work. We're stuck in dead-end fields. Isn't this so since women aren't allowed into the "fast-track" jobs in the market?

Simply because one can find a higher concentration of women in certain positions, it does not necessarily follow that they are being discriminated against. Instead, it may reflect the needs of certain women to choose career paths that allow them flexibility in raising children without significant costs to their careers.

Female Entrepreneurs

In numbers too big to ignore

■ The National Foundation of Women Business Owners found that women own 7.7 million businesses in the United States, employing 15.5 million people and generating $1.4 trillion in sales. Furthermore, women own 3.5 million home-based businesses, employing 5.6 million people full time and 8.4 million workers part time. Those home-based businesses are mainly in service-oriented industries such as consulting.

■ "Women-owned firms are more likely to have remained in business over the past three years than the average U.S. firm."—David T. Kresge, Dunn & Bradstreet Information Services

■ "Women-owned businesses are growing more rapidly than is the overall economy and are major contributors to the nation's economic health and competitiveness."—Laura Henderson, Chair, National Foundation of Women Business Owners

■ The first National Women's Economic Summit, held in May 1996 at Northwestern University, found: "The American economy has been revitalized in good measure because of the participation of and contributions of women business-owners."

■ Given present gains, levels of accomplishments, and rates of growth, female entrepreneurship will continue to flourish, and women business owners will become an even more important force in the economy.

Q & A

Why do women-owned businesses still receive only a small number of government contracts?

Government tends to offer contracts to large businesses; women-owned businesses tend to be smaller. Government contracts tend to be in areas like construction and weapons-building, where there are smaller proportions of women-owned businesses. Most women-owned businesses are concentrated in the service sector.

Introduction

This monograph analyzes women's condition in American society and challenges some enduring assumptions about women's social and economic progress. The study makes no effort or claim to be exhaustive in the topics it covers or the information presented for each topic; instead, it presents data that illustrate the difficulty in constructing plausible—much less conclusive—evidence from market outcomes to support claims that American women are second-class citizens.

The study also gives a statistical rendering of the often-neglected historical record of women's progress. An examination of historical patterns in voting, marriage, education, employment, and other areas reveals the momentous though gradual changes that have taken place in American society. The authors have tried to provide figures from 1920 up to the present. They believe the year 1920 is an excellent starting point for mapping women's progress, for it was in that year, with the passage of the Nineteenth Amendment to the Constitution, that women achieved the right to vote. Since then, American women have achieved a great deal more.

One hundred years ago, American women were an unequal class in American society, complete with unequal laws, unequal schools, unequal access to political institutions, and unequal access to many markets.[1] Women not only were excluded from some labor markets, but also were not allowed to own some forms of property. To find the causes of the inequality of women was simple: one needed to look no further than to federal, state, and local statutes, which in turn engendered unequal attitudes and expectations. Despite those statutes, however, many women ran farms on the frontier and participated actively in nineteenth-century life.

The twentieth century has witnessed many changes to the legal, social, and economic status of women. The inequality of institutions that characterized the

---

[1] A market provides the opportunity for willing buyers and sellers to exchange products.

early years of the century have largely vanished. Legal barriers to women's entering and participating fully in markets have been removed. In their stead, equality of opportunity reigns. Employers in the United States may not engage in sex discrimination involving unequal pay for equal work or in discriminatory hiring or promotion practices.[2] Numerous court cases have upheld the statutes. In *Price Waterhouse* v. *Hopkins*, the Supreme Court ruled that Ann Hopkins, who had been denied a partnership at a major accounting firm, had been the subject of unfair discrimination. While some wage discrimination may persist, it does not appear to be pervasive in the American economy. The equality of opportunity that now exists is the result only partly of government intervention to remove legal barriers; it is also the result of nongovernmental forces such as changes in social attitudes that have come with time, changes in technology, and markets' reacting to those changes.

Markets are at their most efficient with equality of opportunity. Without equality of opportunity for market participants, market outcomes are not truly competitive. Competition has led generations of Americans to strive for greater achievements not because outcomes were guaranteed to be the same, but because competition rewards effort, ingenuity, and capability regardless of the demographic characteristics of the participants. Competitive markets yield the greatest innovations and the most benefits for both consumers and producers. Competitive markets, however, will lead to equality of outcome for market participants only if they are truly identical in all respects. Identical outcomes are impossible in competitive markets to the extent that people differ.

Thus, equality of opportunity in America has not necessarily translated into identical market outcomes for women and men. Some market-oriented observers of the status of women in America find nothing unnatural, unsettling, or unexpected in a wide range of disparate outcomes resulting from equal opportunity in free and competitive markets. Those observers do not see unequal outcomes as the necessary consequence of discrimination. Instead, they point to an array of market and other explanations ranging from a transition from former discriminatory practices to differences in experience, education,

---

[2] Equal Pay Act of 1963 and Title VII of the Civil Rights Act of 1964.

and skills, as well as to differences in preferences, motivations, and expectations as reasons to expect nonidentical outcomes.

According to those market advocates, *equal opportunity* should be the primary policy objective of government, since federal, state, and local governments currently provide American women with sufficient equal opportunity protections through a complex web of statutes and regulations. While isolated instances of sex discrimination occur, available statutes can remedy any harm. To those observers, American women—and, indeed, all Americans—benefit most from equal economic opportunity to participate in free and open competitive markets without further intrusion from the government.

But other observers of the status of women in America see differences in outcomes as the failure rather than the efficiency of markets. They do not believe that market outcomes should necessarily be the product of free exchange between buyers and sellers, and they see the nonidentical outcomes of men and women in the U.S. markets as the result of a sinister system that is inherently unfair to women and in need of further government market intervention. Some claim that the failure to reach *equality of outcome* is evidence that opportunities are, in fact, not yet equal, that current legal remedies are inadequate, and that further government intervention is necessary.[3] Such observations have led to the claim that equality of outcome, rather than equality of opportunity, should be the goal for public policy and consequently further government intervention is needed.

Still other observers claim that the failure to reach equality of outcome reflects the fact that women are victims of their social condition.[4] According to

---

[3] This is clearly the position adopted by the National Association of Women Business Owners, despite the obvious gains made by women in business. In an open letter released last year to Governor Pete Wilson of California, the NAWBO argued that women still lacked the opportunities available to men; see "Let's Stop the Affirmative Action Misinformation Campaign," open letter to Pete Wilson, June 8, 1995, *PR Newswire*. Feminist leader Gloria Steinem, as recently as February 1996, claimed that expanded affirmative action policies are necessary to "rescue women who have fallen into a river of discrimination." See Karen De Witt, "Feminists Gather to Affirm the Relevancy of Their Movement," *New York Times*, Saturday, February 3, 1996.

[4] For a good analysis of this issue, as well as the debate between "gender feminism" and "equity feminism," see Christina Hoff Sommers, *Who Stole Feminism?* (New York: Simon

those claims, women do not fully benefit from equal opportunity because many women accept social stereotypes that determine their preferences, motivations, and expectations. Thus, American women are denied the same rights, privileges, and opportunities as men as a consequence of American socialization. The suggested remedy is considerable government intervention on behalf of women.

Finally, there are those who claim that a failure to reach equality of outcomes for men and women in America is simply an artifact of market failure. Specifically, the market does not reward women with their rightful wage. Those market skeptics fail to recognize the legitimacy of simple market differences; instead, their common theme is that currently available legal remedies are inadequate and that further government intervention is necessary.[5]

A sampling of recent statements from some organizations gives the impression that American women are locked in a losing battle with men in almost all areas of society.[6] According to those groups, women suffer from lower wages, compulsory occupational segregation, and the burden of a "glass ceiling," to name just a few. But the story of the evolution of American markets shows that women are closing the gap. That we discuss in the following section. After showing how poverty disproportionately affects women in the third section, we describe standards of evidence for sex discrimination and show why those standards ought to be higher for the indirect evidence proffered by the current advocates of women as victims. The final section provides the conclusion.

and Schuster, 1994); also see Gertrude Himmelfarb's review of Sommers, "A Sentimental Priesthood," *Times Literary Supplement*, November 11, 1994; and Irving Kristol, "Sex Trumps Gender," *Wall Street Journal*, Wednesday, March 6, 1996.

[5] A market skeptic holds the view that women's outcomes are the result of discrimination rather than economic supply and demand characteristics.

[6] See, for example, Eleanor Smeal, as quoted in Kevin Merida, "Feminist Expo '96 Billed as Rebirth of the Women's Movement," *Washington Post*, February 4, 1996, p. A22.

Women Are Closing the Gap

Most recent data indicate that women are closing the formerly wide gulfs that separated them from men in terms of economic, social, and educational status. This section examines the narrowing of gaps between the sexes in wages, educational achievement, labor force participation, occupational choices, and election to public office.

■ Wages

Women are closing the gap with men in wages and income levels. In the 1960s, protesters wore "59¢" buttons to publicize the fact that women allegedly earned only fifty-nine cents for every dollar earned by a male. Today, some groups such as the National Organization for Women (NOW) claim that women are still punished with lower wages, earning somewhere between sixty to eighty-nine cents for every dollar earned by a male. Those claims fail to recognize the multiple factors that affect income levels.

Employment compensation is perhaps the bloodiest battleground in the wars between the sexes. It is also the area in which the most blatant distortion of statistics has occurred. In particular, two rhetorical devices loom large over nearly every report on the subject of employment compensation: the "wage gap" and the "glass ceiling." Cited constantly by those skeptical of market outcomes, those popular mantras have been used to argue that income inequality between the sexes is the direct result of discrimination on the part of employers and that government intervention is the only way to rectify that injustice. The statistics and arguments deployed as evidence for the existence of both the "wage gap" and the "glass ceiling" do not, however, withstand close examination.

■ The Wage Gap

Frequently cited as evidence of sex discrimination in employment compensation is the "wage gap." In *Facts on Working Women*, the U.S. Department of Labor reports that the ratio of women's median weekly earnings to men's is 76.4 percent.[7] Even in traditionally female occupations, where women outnumber men, women still earn less than men. That is a disturbing figure, but how was it calculated? What does it really tell us about income differences?

Economist June O'Neill has argued that such numbers, removed from their context, tell us little about the existence of discrimination, for they do not take into consideration important determinants of income, such as lifetime education and work experience. A U.S. Department of Labor study concludes that the existence and effect of discrimination "on the earnings gap [are] hard to measure,"[8] and data demonstrate that between 1920 and 1980 women's wages grew at a rate 20 percent faster than men's wages.[9]

Even though discrimination is frequently blamed for income differentials, a host of choices made by men and women—personal choices made *outside* the work environment—have important implications for men's and women's earnings. Those choices often have a negative effect on pensions, promotions, and total wages.

Recent economic literature on choices made by women in the working world emphasizes that multiple forces in the market play an important part in determining compensation. Occupation, seniority, absenteeism, and intermittent work-force participation are all critical variables in accounting for pay disparities. In other words, those who assume that discrimination is solely to blame for wage differences are drawing unsubstantiated conclusions. The issue is far more complex.

Decisions that affect seniority and absenteeism are particularly important to

---

[7] U.S. Department of Labor, *Facts on Working Women*, no. 95-1 (Washington, D.C.: Government Printing Office, May 1995).

[8] Ibid.

[9] U.S. Department of Labor, *1993 Handbook on Women Workers* (Washington, D.C.: Government Printing Office, 1993), p. 27.

understand. For example, a higher percentage of women's work years are spent away from work, owing to childbearing and family responsibilities.[10] Hence, women's opportunities for promotion may not be so great as those of their male colleagues. That in itself is not evidence of discrimination, but of personal decisions made by women. Sally Pipes, an economist and president of the Pacific Research Institute for Public Policy, has suggested that many women do not want to reach parity at the highest levels of the corporate world. She cited a recent study by Korn/Ferry that found only 14 percent of women surveyed aspiring to reach the position of CEO, compared with 46 percent of the men surveyed.[11] A 1992 management study cited by the *Economist* reached a similar conclusion. It suggested not only that men "work more hours than women and spend more years in the workforce," but that "women were one-third as likely (14 percent to 44 percent) as men to aspire to be top dog."[12]

It is likely that women, who are most frequently children's primary caregivers, take the responsibilities of motherhood into consideration when making employment decisions. Thus, as we noted earlier, many women, planning to interrupt their careers at some point in the future to have children, choose fields where job flexibility is high, salaries are lower, and job skills deteriorate at a slower rate than others. Furthermore, men and women choose different fields of study, which result in different income levels after graduation. Since that is the case, comparing incomes by the highest degree earned does not measure discrimination and produces numbers that are politically useful but meaningless in practice.[13] Given those educational and career choices, comparing the *average* wages of men and women is not a comparison of like units. It is another misleading comparison.

Figures 1, 2, and 3 show estimates of the ratio of women's to men's earnings in three different age groups from a data series constructed by David

---

[10] U.S. Bureau of the Census, *Current Population Reports*, Series P-70, no. 10 (Washington, D.C.: Government Printing Office, 1987).

[11] Sally Pipes, "Glass Ceiling? So What?" *Chief Executive*, April 1996.

[12] Sally Pipes, "Through a Glass, Darkly," *Economist*, August 10, 1996.

[13] Katherine Post and Michael Lynch, "Free Markets, Free Choices: Women in the Workforce," Pacific Research Institute, December 11, 1995.

FIGURE 1

Estimated Earnings of Women Ages 16–29 as a Percentage of
Men's Earnings, Controlling for Demographic and
Job Characteristics
1974–1993

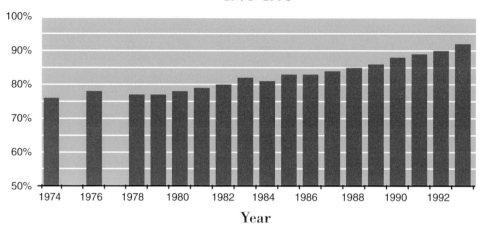

Year

Note: This estimate accounts for education, race, age, part- or full-time, public- or private-sector status, production or non-production occupation, and union status. Data for 1975 and 1977 are not available.

Source: David A. Macpherson and Barry T. Hirsch, "Wages and Gender Composition: Why Do Women's Jobs Pay Less?" *Journal of Labor Economics*, vol. 13 (July 1995): p. 466, table A1.

MacPherson and Barry Hirsch.[14] They control for education, age, race, part- or full-time status, private- and public-sector status, production and nonproduction occupational status, and union status. We can see that women's wages have been steadily rising relative to men's wages in all age groups over the period 1974 to 1993. The greatest gains for women have been in the youngest age group, age sixteen to twenty-nine, for whom wages rose from 74 percent to 92 percent over that period, as shown in figure 1. It is significant that the younger the age group, the higher the wage relative to men's. The *National Longitudinal Survey of Youth* found an even smaller gap between men's and women's earnings: among people ages twenty-seven to thirty-three who have never had a child, women's earnings are close to 98 percent of men's.[15] As June

---

[14] David A. Macpherson and Barry T. Hirsch, "Wages and Gender Composition: Why Do Women's Jobs Pay Less?" *Journal of Labor Economics*, vol. 13, July 1995, pp. 426–71.

[15] June O'Neill, "The Shrinking Pay Gap," *Wall Street Journal*, October 7, 1994.

FIGURE 2

Estimated Earnings of Women Ages 30–40 as a Percentage of Men's Earnings, Controlling for Demographic and Job Characteristics 1974–1993

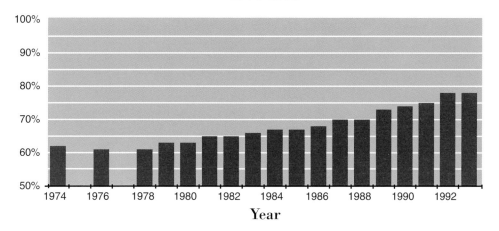

Note: This estimate accounts for education, race, age, part- or full-time, public- or private-sector status, production or non-production occupation, and union status. Data for 1975 and 1977 are not available.

Source: David A. Macpherson and Barry T. Hirsch, "Wages and Gender Composition: Why Do Women's Jobs Pay Less?" *Journal of Labor Economics*, vol. 13 (July 1995): p. 466, table A1.

FIGURE 3

Estimated Earnings of Women Ages 45 and Older as a Percentage of Men's Earnings, Controlling for Demographic and Job Characteristics 1974–1993

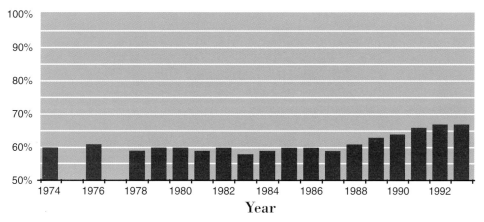

Note: This estimate accounts for education, race, age, part- or full-time, public- or private-sector status, production or non-production occupation, and union status. Data for 1975 and 1977 are not available.

Source: David A. Macpherson and Barry T. Hirsch, "Wages and Gender Composition: Why Do Women's Jobs Pay Less?" *Journal of Labor Economics*, vol. 13 (July 1995): p. 466, table A1.

O'Neill notes, "When earnings comparisons are restricted to men and women more similar in their experience and life situations, the measured earnings differentials are typically quite small."[16]

Yet some continue to promote discrimination as the primary cause of earnings differences between men and women. In January 1996 the *New York Times* reported on an American Bar Association study that purported to show setbacks for women lawyers. The study showed that despite the visible inroads women have made into the profession, they continue to face lower rates of promotion and lower wages than their male counterparts, and concluded that discrimination was still rampant in law offices nationwide.

Included in the study, however, were some quotations from women lawyers that bear closer scrutiny. The study noted that those women lawyers "say that they are less willing to make extreme personal sacrifices" and that they "expect employers to accommodate their life needs," including having children.[17] What this shows, then, is that some women lawyers have made choices regarding priorities that might ultimately have a negative effect on their professional success. If a lawyer is expected to work a consistent sixty-hour week to become a partner, then a woman or man who requests scaled-back hours cannot expect to be promoted at the same rate. What appears to be happening (and what is ignored by those who cite discrimination) is that women in many professions are making decisions about work and family priorities that can result in fewer women's reaching the top of their fields.

That trend is rarely recognized by those who measure success solely by women's performance in the professional world. Nonwork factors frequently assume equal importance: a Department of Labor study found that "63 percent of mothers with children age five and under gave high priority to getting paid leave to care for children."[18] Those women recognized that caring for their

---

16 Ibid.

17 Nina Bernstein, "Equal Opportunity Recedes for Most Female Lawyers," *New York Times*, January 8, 1996.

18 U.S. Department of Labor, "Executive Summary," *Working Women Count: A Report to the Nation* (Washington, D.C.: Government Printing Office, 1994).

children meant higher rates of absenteeism and thus fewer opportunities for promotions—a trade-off they were willing to make.

Many mothers, including unmarried mothers, often work to help support their families. It may be unfair that the bulk of childcare responsibilities continues to fall to mothers rather than to fathers, but it is not clear that most women see motherhood as a burden. According to Elizabeth Fox-Genovese, "Even highly successful women frequently want to spend much more time with their young children than the sixty-hour weeks required by the corporate fast tracks will permit."[19] The quandary many women face when they combine work and motherhood is a painful one, but it is a matter of choices made by individuals. Women are not the only ones making such choices: an increasing number of men are changing the schedules of their professional lives to have more time with their families. Although the consequences of those individual choices are sometimes negative for women's professional lives, that is not in itself evidence of discrimination.

[19] Elizabeth Fox-Genovese, *Feminism Is Not the Story of My Life* (New York: Doubleday, 1996).

■ The Existence of the "Glass Ceiling"

Does the "glass ceiling" exist? Are American women systematically denied access to the upper echelons of professions simply because they are women? The *glass ceiling* was a term coined by the *Wall Street Journal* in 1986 to describe the "invisible but impenetrable barrier between women and the executive suite." It is alleged that the glass ceiling, like occupational segregation, prevents women from attaining the more lucrative positions.

The Civil Rights Act of 1991 created a Glass Ceiling Commission charged with monitoring and reporting on the diversity of the American workplace. The commission in 1995 released a report that has since become gospel to those claiming victim status for women. It ominously concluded that only 5 percent of senior managers at *Fortune* 2000 industrial and service companies are women, implying that systematic discrimination was the cause.[20]

Yet an assessment of the Glass Ceiling Commission's methods raises questions about that 5 percent figure. Typical qualifications for corporate senior management positions include both an MBA and twenty-five years of work experience. The logical sequence of questions the commission should ask would be, first, What percentage of women meets these requirements? and, second, Of that group of qualified women, what proportion has made it to the upper ranks of corporate America? By comparing the number of women qualified to hold top executive positions with the number actually in those positions, one could make some conclusions about the existence of a "glass ceiling."

Those are not the questions the Glass Ceiling Commission asked, however. Instead, it compared the number of women in the total labor force, without reference to experience or education levels, with the number wielding power at *Fortune* 2000 companies. That comparison results in a statistically corrupt but rhetorically and politically useful figure of 5 percent. In its refusal to use the qualified labor pool in its assessment, the commission reached alarming but highly misleading conclusions about women's employment opportunities.

---

[20] Federal Glass Ceiling Commission, *Good for Business: Making Full Use of the Nation's Human Capital* (Washington, D.C.: Government Printing Office, March 1995).

A cursory glance at the history of professional school degrees reveals that very few of the graduates of the 1950s and 1960s, who today would be at the pinnacles of their professions, were women. That lends support to the "pipeline" theory, which holds that women have not made it to the top in some professions simply because they have not been "in the pipeline" long enough to gain the requisite experience. In addition, since entering the work force in significant numbers, women have also steadily increased their numbers in "male-dominated" professions, as illustrated in figure 4. Critics attack the pipeline theory as an excuse for ignoring discrimination in the workplace, but women's gains in the American economy (as the section on women in business reveals) and in the corporate world show that the pipeline theory remains the most viable explanation for women's progress. The Korn/Ferry executive search firm found in a recent study that, during the past decade, the number of female executive vice-presidents more than doubled and the number of female senior vice-presidents increased by 75 percent. Yet critics of the pipeline theory ignore that remarkable growth, choosing instead to focus only on the number of women in CEO positions.

FIGURE 4

Women as a Percentage of Total Employment by Occupation
1983 and 1995

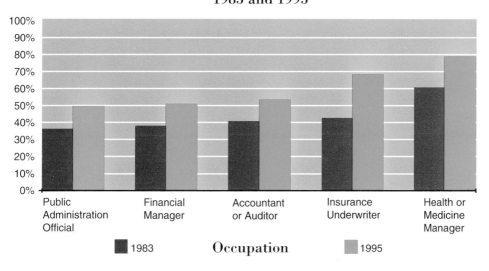

Source: U.S. Bureau of Labor Statistics, unpublished tabulation from the *Current Population Survey*.

Finally, it is worth noting that the qualification for success used by the Glass Ceiling Commission was achievement in a *Fortune* 2000 company. *Fortune* 2000 companies are only one portion of the market. Given recent evidence of the success of women-owned businesses and women in small business, the conclusions of the committee say little about women's participation in the economy as a *whole*.

As the above discussion has demonstrated, both the *glass ceiling* and the *wage gap* are rhetorically powerful but factually bankrupt terms. Those who insist on invoking those concepts as *evidence* of discrimination encourage unnecessary and harmful government intervention. Individual cases of discrimination still occur in the workplace, but laws prohibiting discrimination have been in existence for thirty years and should continue to be rigorously enforced. Those occurrences should not, however, be cited as evidence of rampant discrimination. What needs to be recognized, as Katherine Post and Michael Lynch have suggested, is that "in today's world it is not pervasive and systemic discrimination but a myriad of decisions and considerations—personal choices—that determine a person's role in the marketplace."[21] Furthermore, salary levels are not the only consideration for workers. Flexibility, work setting, and job interest are important to both men and women.

If there is evidence of market discrimination against either men or women, it is not easily revealed in unemployment statistics either. Figure 5 presents the unemployment rates for men and women between 1940 and 1995. Rates rarely have diverged by much, and since 1980, they have never diverged by as much as a percentage point.

---

[21] Katherine Post and Michael Lynch, "Smoke and Mirrors: Women and the Glass Ceiling," *Pacific Research Institute Fact Sheet*, November 1995.

FIGURE 5

Unemployment Rates by Sex
1940–1995

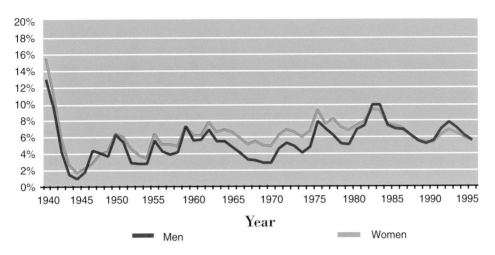

Year

Men   Women

Note: Data beginning in 1994 are not directly comparable with earlier years. Data for 1940–1947 include ages 14 and older; data since 1947 include ages 16 and older.

Sources: *Historical Statistics,* vol. 1, Series D, pp. 11–25; *Statistical Abstract:* 1950, no. 209; 1977, no. 627; 1979, no. 647; 1988, no. 647; 1991, no. 635; 1994, no. 616; 1995, no. 628.

■ Educational Attainment and Educational Choices

At the beginning of the twentieth century, education, and particularly higher education, was aimed primarily at men. Many schools and colleges were exclusively for men. Many of the professions for which college provided preparation—such as divinity, law, medicine, and engineering—were by common practice (if not by law) restricted to men. Figures 6 through 9 illustrate the steadily growing percentage of associate, college, and graduate degrees awarded to women in the United States since 1920 (data for associate degrees begin in 1966).[22] Today the majority of associate, bachelor's, and master's degrees are

---

[22] During World War II, there was a short-lived increase in the percentage of graduates who were women as most university-aged men were in the armed services.

awarded to women, and nearly 40 percent of doctorates are conferred to women.

Women have made considerable gains in education. Not only are they represented in greater numbers at the college and postgraduate levels; they have also steadily been entering traditionally male-dominated programs. In 1996 women represent 54 percent of the class admitted to Yale Medical School. In 1994 women earned more associate, bachelor's, and master's degrees than men. According to data from the Department of Labor, women have outnumbered men in graduate school since the mid-1980s.[23] Figure 10 charts the dramatic increase in the percentage of first professional degrees awarded to women from 5 percent as recently as 1970 to over 40 percent in 1994. Figures 11 through 13 show a similar pattern of the women's share of degrees awarded in each of the specific professional fields of law, dentistry, and medicine.

FIGURE 6

**Percentage of Associate Degrees Awarded to Women
1966–1994**

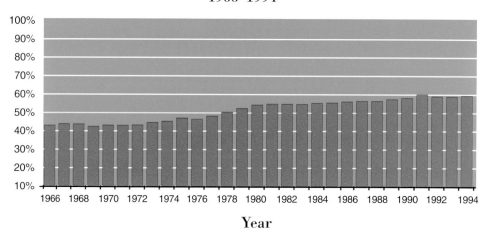

Source: U.S. Department of Education, National Center for Education Statistics, Integrated Post-Secondary Education Data System, "Completions" surveys.

---

[23] U.S. Department of Labor, *1993 Handbook on Women Workers*, p. 89.

FIGURE 7

Percentage of Bachelor's Degrees Awarded to Women
1920–1994

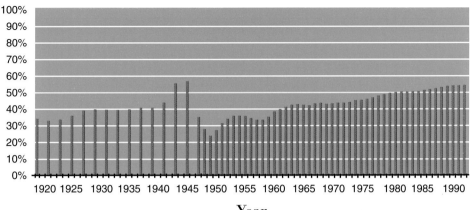

Note: Data for odd years from 1921 to 1947 are not available.

Source: U.S. Department of Education, National Center for Education Statistics, Integrated Post-Secondary Education Data System, "Completions" surveys.

FIGURE 8

Percentage of Master's Degrees Awarded to Women
1920–1994

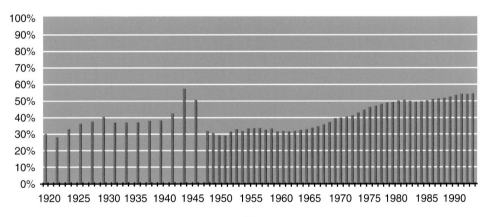

Note: Data for odd years from 1921 to 1947 are not available.

Source: U.S. Department of Education, National Center for Education Statistics, Integrated Post-Secondary Education Data System, "Completions" surveys.

FIGURE 9

Percentage of Doctorate Degrees Awarded to Women
1920–1994

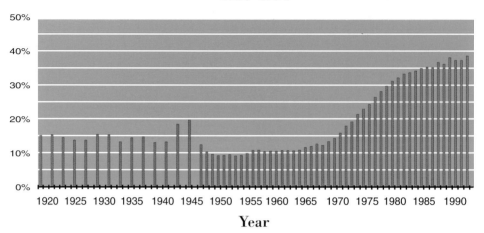

Note: Data for odd years from 1921 to 1947 are not available.

Source: U.S. Department of Education, National Center for Education Statistics, Integrated Post-Secondary Education Data System, "Completions" surveys.

FIGURE 10

Percentage of First Professional Degrees Awarded to Women
1961–1994

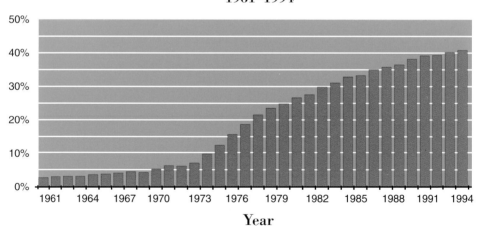

Note: First professional degrees are defined as requiring at least two years of college and a total of six years of schooling and certify an individual to practice a particular profession. First professional degrees are conferred in the fields of chiropractic medicine, dentistry, law, medicine, optometry, osteopathic medicine, pharmacy, podiatry, theology, and veterinary medicine.

Source: U.S. Department of Education, National Center for Educational Statistics, Integrated Post-Secondary Education Data Systems, "Completions" surveys.

FIGURE 11

Percentage of Law Degrees Awarded to Women
1956–1994

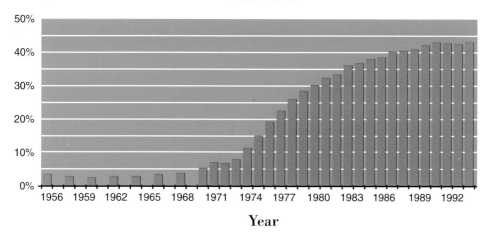

Note: Data for odd years from 1957 to 1969 are not available.

Source: U.S. Department of Education, National Center for Education Studies, "Degrees and Other Formal Awards Conferred" surveys and Integrated Post-Secondary Education Data System, "Completions" surveys.

FIGURE 12

Percentage of Dentistry Degrees Awarded to Women
1950–1994

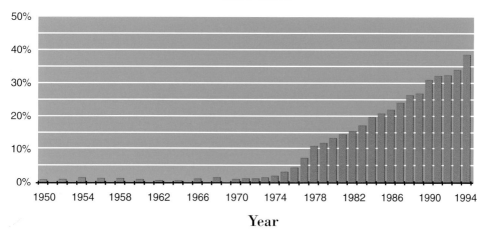

Note: Data for odd years from 1951 to 1969 are not available.

Source: U.S. Department of Education, National Center for Education Studies, "Degrees and Other Formal Awards Conferred" surveys and Integrated Post-Secondary Education Data System, "Completions" surveys.

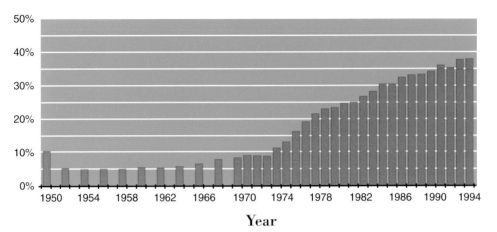

FIGURE 13

Percentage of Medical Degrees Awarded to Women
1950–1994

Year

Note: Data for odd years from 1951 to 1969 are not available.

Source: U.S. Department of Education, National Center for Education Studies, "Degrees and Other Formal Awards Conferred" surveys and Integrated Post-Secondary Education Data System, "Completions" surveys.

■ Labor Force Participation

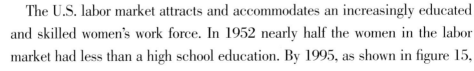

The labor force participation rate refers to the proportion of the population that either is employed or is seeking to be employed. Outside the labor market are homemakers, retirees, the chronically ill, and others who simply are not seeking employment. The higher educational attainment of women is related to increased participation in the U.S. labor market, since increased labor market opportunities also encourage women to pursue further education. As shown in figure 14, female labor force participation increased from 26 percent in 1940 to 59 percent in 1995. Moreover, in the 1990s, more than 70 percent of women between the ages of twenty and fifty-four are in the labor force. Working in the market economy rather than in the home has shifted from being the exception to being the norm for American women.

The U.S. labor market attracts and accommodates an increasingly educated and skilled women's work force. In 1952 nearly half the women in the labor market had less than a high school education. By 1995, as shown in figure 15,

FIGURE 14

Percentage of Women in the Labor Force
1940–1995

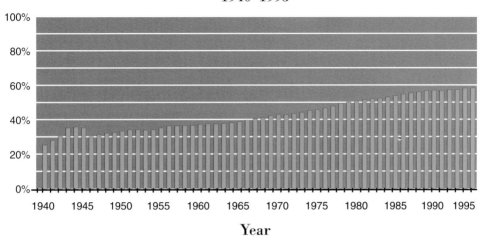

Source: *Handbook of Labor Statistics*, 1988, table 5; *Historical Statistics*, vol.1, Series A, pp. 119–134, Series D, pp. 29–41; *Statistical Abstract*: 1994, no. 615; 1993, no. 622; 1988, no. 625; and *Employment and Earnings*, vol. 43, no. 1, annual averages, table 3.

FIGURE 15

Distribution of Female Labor Force by Educational Attainment
1952–1995

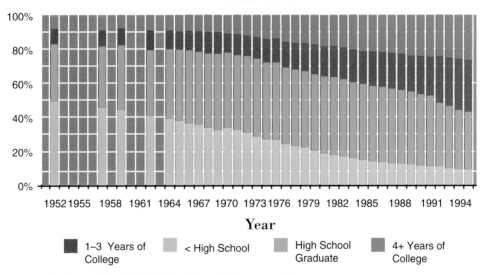

| 1–3 Years of College | < High School | High School Graduate | 4+ Years of College |

Note: Data for 1953–1956, 1958, 1960–1961, and 1963 are not available.

Sources: *Statistical Abstract*: 1991, no. 634; 1994, no. 617. *Handbook of Labor Statistics*: 1967, table 8; 1985, table 61; 1989, table 65. Bureau of Labor Statistics, unpublished data from the *Current Population Survey*, annual averages, 1992, 1993, 1994, and 1995.

only 9 percent of women in the work force had less than a high school education, and nearly *half* the women in the labor market had attended at least one year of college. While dramatic, the change in the educational attainment of women in the labor force over the past few decades differs little from the change for men. Consequently, the increased labor force participation rate of women over the same time period reflects market, social, and technological factors rather than just changes in education.

The number of women in the U.S. labor force has grown much more rapidly in recent years than has the number of men. As shown in figure 16, the number of women in the work force, either part-time or full-time employees, grew by 100 percent between 1968 and 1995. In contrast, the number of men in the labor force grew by only 30 percent during the same period. Figures 17 and 18 show that women's employment has nearly doubled in both full-time and part-time labor markets. Thus, the increased employment of women is not merely an artifact of increased use of part-time employees.

Many researchers have suggested that technological changes have made household management and maintenance less time-consuming, enabling mil-

FIGURE 16

**Total Employment by Sex
1968–1995**

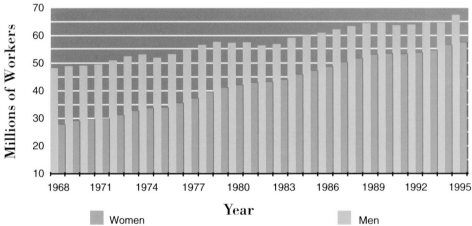

Women   Men

Note: Data for 1994 and 1995 are not strictly comparable with prior years owing to the introduction of a redesigned *Current Population Survey* questionnaire.

Source: U.S. Bureau of the Census, *Current Population Survey*.

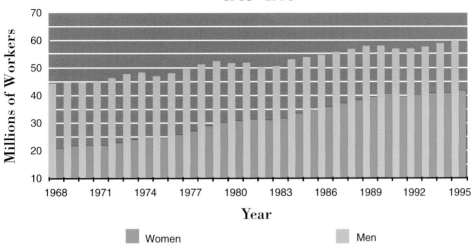

FIGURE 17

Full-Time Employment by Sex
1968 –1995

Note: Data for 1994 and 1995 are not strictly comparable with prior years owing to the introduction of a redesigned *Current Population Survey* questionnaire.

Source: U.S. Bureau of the Census, *Current Population Survey.*

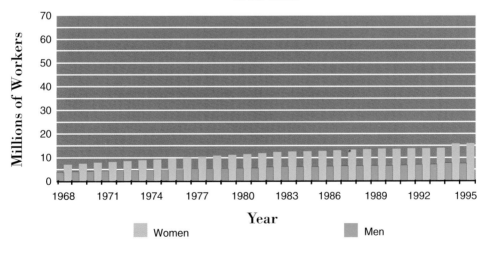

FIGURE 18

Part-Time Employment by Sex
1968–1995

Note: Data for 1994 and 1995 are not strictly comparable with prior years owing to the introduction of a redesigned *Current Population Survey* questionnaire.

Source: U.S. Bureau of the Census, *Current Population Survey.*

lions engaged in household activities, primarily women, to enter the market labor force and to work more hours. According to a study of how Americans use their time conducted by Thomas Juster, director of the University of Michigan's Institute for Social Research, the amount of time women devote to housework has declined substantially: "Women 25 to 44 years old spent 46 hours a week doing housework in 1965 but devoted only 35 hours a week to household chores 10 years later."[24]

The greatest increase in women's labor force participation has occurred among married women. In 1920 only 9 percent of married women were in the labor force, and, as late as 1950, fewer than 25 percent of married women participated. As figure 19 shows, that number had risen to more than 60 percent by 1995. Increased employment among married women has not left families

FIGURE 19

Percentage of Women in the Labor Force by Marital Status 1947–1995

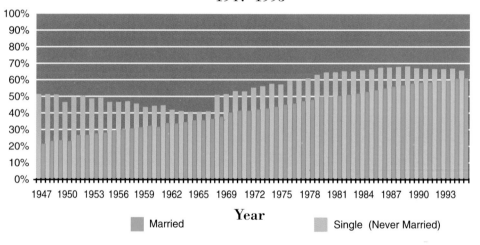

Notes: Data are for 1947–1966, including women 14 years old and older. Beginning in 1967, all data refer to women ages 16 and older. Single teenagers not in the labor force may be in school.

Sources: *Historical Statistics*, vol.1, Series D, pp. 49–62; *Statistical Abstract:* 1995, no. 637; 1981, no. 652; and the U.S. Bureau of Labor Statistics, unpublished tabulations from the *Current Population Survey*, March 1995.

[24] Quoted in Nick Jordan, "Labors Neither Loved Nor Lost: Changing Perceptions of Housework," *Psychology Today*, vol. 19, October 1985, p. 70.

unaffected. What about the often-touted goal of having both career and family? A 1995 study by Claudia Goldin, a research associate at the National Bureau of Economic Research, found that only about 15 percent of women questioned who received college degrees around 1972 were maintaining both career and family. Among those who have had a successful career, as indicated by income level, nearly 50 percent were childless.[25]

■ Occupational Choices

The steady entrance of women into previously male-dominated educational programs has resulted in greater numbers of women entering and succeeding in traditionally male-dominated professions. Although Goldin shows that 1972 graduates were less successful at managing both career and family, more recent graduates are increasingly combining the two. A recent Korn/Ferry study of corporate executives in America found that, in the past ten years, the number of female executive vice-presidents more than doubled, and the number of female senior vice-presidents increased by 75 percent.[26] Furthermore, Department of Labor data suggest that, given current trends in education and job experience, women can expect to hold as much as 15 percent of the top executive positions in *Fortune* 1000 companies in the near future.[27]

But some observers see those results only as further evidence that women are victims of discrimination in the labor market. Most women, they argue, will never even have the opportunity to reach the business world because they are deliberately segregated into lower-paying jobs in the labor market. Such "occupational segregation" supposedly prevents women from entering higher-paying fields.

---

[25] Claudia Goldin, "Career and Family: College Women Look to the Past," NBER Working Paper No. 5188; cited in the *National Bureau of Economic Research Digest*, December 1995.

[26] Sally Pipes, "Glass Ceiling? So What?"

[27] U.S. Department of Labor, *1993 Handbook on Women Workers*.

A standard definition of occupational segregation, according to Andrea H. Beller in the *Journal of Human Resources*, states that "if more than half the population is denied access to 60 percent of the occupations, being crowded into a few at lower earnings, equality of opportunity does not exist."[28] Beller notes that "if women freely choose to enter only a third of all occupations and those occupations pay less, then women's lower earnings may not be a fundamental social problem."[29] The primary issue centers around the choices made by men and women in the labor market. Do those differences in occupational distributions occur because of personal choices made in an environment of equal opportunity or, as those who tout women's victimhood claim, in an environment of unequal opportunity and limited choice? In other words, is it plausible to claim that women working in "women's professions," or the "pink ghetto," as it is also called, have freely chosen to be there?

As June O'Neill has pointed out, "Although pay in [typically] women's occupations has been found to be lower than pay in typically male occupations, this fact alone is not evidence of employer discrimination."[30] Many factors contribute to the concentration of women in certain professions, but one of the most important and overlooked is that many "pink-collar" jobs offer much-desired flexibility for working women. Many women are willing to accept substantially lower earnings to have a job with flexible hours.[31] Furthermore, many traditional female jobs require job skills that deteriorate slowly, allowing women to leave the work force for a time—to have children, for example—and still retain the skills needed to be viable job candidates when they return to the work force. In a field such as engineering, for example, where job skills deteriorate rapidly, that would not be possible. Over time, occupational segregation

---

[28] Andrea H. Beller, "Occupational Segregation by Sex: Determinants and Changes," *Journal of Human Resources*, Summer 1982.

[29] Ibid.

[30] June O'Neill, "Comparable Worth," *Fortune Encyclopedia of Economics*, edited by David R. Henderson (New York: Warner Books, 1993).

[31] Wendy Leé Gramm, "Household Utility Maximization and the Working Wife," *American Economic Review*, vol. 65, March 1975, pp. 90–100.

has diminished and will continue to diminish.[32] Women continue to enter and succeed in "male-dominated" professions, a trend that is the result of women's increased presence in certain "male" programs of higher education.

■ Women in Business

Perhaps the most outstanding gains made by women lately have been in the business world. Despite arguments about rampant discrimination and lack of opportunities, women nationwide have been starting their own businesses and succeeding. One reason for that could be that the increased flexibility of self-employment benefits women and motivates success.

Today there are 7.7 million women-owned businesses in the United States, employing 15.5 million people and generating $1.4 trillion in sales. The number of women-owned businesses increased 43 percent from 1987 to 1992.[33] In 1993 the Department of Labor released statistics documenting that women are starting businesses at twice the rate of men.[34] Figure 20 shows the dramatic increase in the number of women-owned businesses from 1972 to 1996.

Women are also starting home-based businesses in record numbers. Data show that women owned 3.5 million of those home businesses, mainly in service-oriented industries like consulting and finance. Such statistics belie the idea that women face a market economy saturated with sex discrimination. As participants in the first National Women's Economic Summit found in May 1996, "The American economy has been revitalized in good measure because of the participation of and contributions of women business-owners."[35]

---

[32] Karen C. Holden and W. Lee Hansen, "Part-Time Work, Full-Time Work, and Occupational Segregation," in Clair Brown and Joseph A. Pechman, eds., *Gender in the Workplace* (Washington, D.C.: Brookings Institution, 1987).

[33] Stephanie Mehta, "Number of Women-Owned Businesses Surged 43% in 5 Years through 1992," *Wall Street Journal*, January 29, 1996.

[34] U.S. Department of Labor, *1993 Handbook on Women Workers*, p. 59.

[35] "A Wealth of Working Women," *Economist*, June 8, 1996, p. 28.

FIGURE 20

Number of Women-Owned Businesses
1972–1996

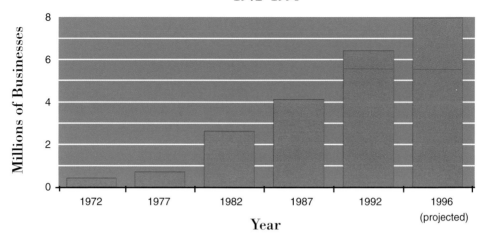

Note: Data for 1992 and 1996 include "C" corporations.

Sources: U.S. Bureau of the Census, *Economic Census,* "Women-Owned Businesses": 1977, table 1; 1987, table 1; 1992, table 1. National Foundation for Women Business Owners, "Women-Owned Businesses in the United States: A Fact Sheet," 1996.

■ Elected Officials

Business is not the only realm in which women are exercising greater influence. They are also entering the political arena, competing for—and winning—elective office. Tables 1 and 2 show the increasing tendency of women in recent years to run in one of the two major political parties for both the U.S. Congress and selected state offices. In 1974, for example, 47 women were candidates of one of the major political parties for Congress; 36 women were candidates for statewide office; and 1,125 women were candidates for state legislature. Twenty years later, more than twice as many women were running for office in one of the major political parties: 121 for Congress, 79 for statewide office, and 2,284 for state legislature. Figure 21 shows the increase in numbers of female congressional candidates from 1968 to 1994.

A recent study by Jody Newman of the National Women's Political Caucus found negligible differences between men and women in success rates in win-

TABLE 1

Summary of Women Candidates
for United States Congressional Offices
1968–1994

Election Year	Senate	House
1968	1 (1D, 0R)	19 (12D, 7R)
1970	1 (0D, 1R)	25 (15D, 10R)
1972	2 (0D, 2R)	32 (24D, 8R)
1974	3 (2D, 1R)	44 (30D, 14R)
1976	1 (1D, 0R)	54 (34D, 20R)
1978	2 (1D, 1R)	46 (27D, 19R)
1980	5 (2D, 3R)	52 (27D, 25R)
1982	3 (1D, 2R)	55 (27D, 28R)
1984	10 (6D, 4R)	65 (30D, 35R)
1986	6 (3D, 3R)	64 (30D, 34R)
1988	2 (0D, 2R)	59 (33D, 26R)
1990	8 (2D, 6R)	69 (39D, 30R)
1992	11 (10D, 1R)	106 (70D, 36R)
1994	9 (4D, 5R)	112 (72D, 40R)

Notes: Data include minor party candidates only if their parties have recently won statewide offices. Data since 1990 do not include the delegates from Washington, D.C., and the five territories.

Source: The Center for the American Woman and Politics, Eagleton Institute of Politics, Rutgers University.

TABLE 2
Summary of Women Candidates
for State Executive and Legislative Offices
1974–1994

Election Year	Governor	Lt. Governor	Secretary of State	State Auditor	State Treasurer	State Legislator
1974	3 (1D, 2R)	4 (1D, 3R)	14 (6D, 8R)	5 (3D, 2R)	10 (8D, 2R)	1,125
1976	2 (2D, 0R)	1 (0D, 1R)	3 (0D, 3R)	0	6 (3D, 3R)	1,258
1978	1 (1D, 0R)	9 (6D, 3R)	16 (9D, 7R)	2 (2D, 0R)	10 (6D, 4R)	1,348
1980	0	3 (2D, 1R)	4 (1D, 3R)	3 (2D, 1R)	3 (2D, 1R)	1,426
1982	2 (2D, 0R)	7 (4D, 3R)	14 (7D, 7R)	1 (1D, 0R)	10 (6D, 4R)	1,643
1984	1 (1D, 0R)	6 (4D, 2R)	6 (4D, 2R)	4 (2D, 2R)	1 (1D, 0R)	1,756
1986	8 (3D, 5R)	11 (6D, 5R)	21 (14D, 7R)	6 (4D, 2R)	11 (7D, 4R)	1,813
1988	2 (2D, 0R)	2 (1D, 1R)	3 (2D, 1R)	2 (0D, 2R)	2 (1D, 1R)	1,853
1990	8 (4D, 4R)	19 (8D, 10R, 1 nd.)	17 (8D, 9R)	7 (5D, 2R)	16 (8D, 8R)	2,064
1992	3 (2D, 1R)	7 (3D, 4R)	5 (3D, 2R)	1 (0D, 1R)	5 (3D, 2R)	2,375
1994	10 (6D, 3R, 1 Ind.)	29 (14D, 13R, 2 Ind.)	20 (8D, 12 R)	4 (1D, 3R)	16 (11D, 5R)	2,284

Notes: Data include minor party candidates only if their parties have recently won statewide offices. Data since 1990 do not include the delegates from Washington, D.C., and the five territories.

Source: The Center for the American Woman and Politics, Eagleton Institute of Politics, Rutgers University.

ning state and national races. In state house elections, for example, women running for open seats won 52 percent of the time, compared to 53 percent of the time for men. In total, the study found no evidence that women had fewer chances to win than men.[36] Similar evidence has been shown by Kellyanne Fitzpatrick.[37] That is not a minor point. Claims of society-wide discrimination against women sound increasingly more hollow when it is shown that voting members of that society choose female candidates as often as they choose male candidates. Those similar success rates suggest that what matters are issues and a candidate's ability to tackle them, regardless of sex. Women are likely to continue to enter the political arena, representing the full range of perspectives and philosophies.

FIGURE 21

Number of Women Candidates
for United States Congressional Offices
1968 –1994

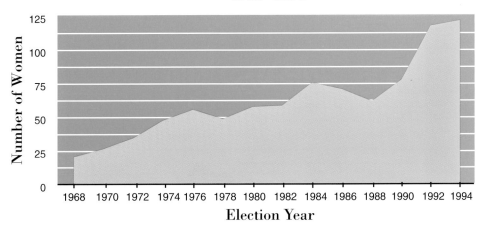

Notes: Data include minor party candidates only if their parties have recently won statewide offices. Data after 1990 do not include the delegates from Washington, D.C., and the five territories.

Source: The Center for the American Woman and Politics, Eagleton Institute of Politics, Rutgers University.

---

[36] Reported in Karlyn Bowman, "The Gender Factor," *America at the Polls, 1994* (Storrs, Conn.: Roper Center for Public Opinion Research, 1995).

[37] Kellyanne Fitzpatrick, "Beyond the Gender Gap," *Wall Street Journal*, May 17, 1996, p. A14.

Figure 22 and table 3 show the number of women in Congress since the 66th Congress in 1919. Until 1981, no more than twenty women had served in Congress at one time. Today, 8 of 100 senators are women, and 47 of 435 representatives are women. Although the number of elected women government officials remains small relative to men, the increasing numbers do reveal a gradual acceptance of women's place in national government. Women have also been increasing their numbers in state legislatures and in state executive offices. According to the Center for the American Woman and Politics, in 1996 21 percent of state legislators are women, compared with 4 percent in 1969. Women represented 26 percent of statewide elected officials. The Center for the American Woman and Politics reported 1,341 female winners in state legislative races in 1994.

FIGURE 22

Number of Women in the United States Congress
1919–1995

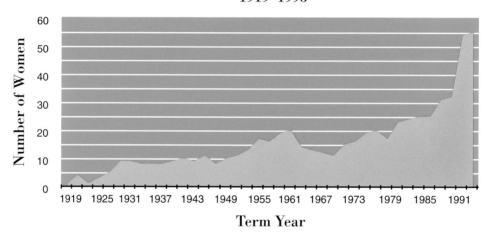

Notes: Table shows maximum number of women elected or appointed to serve in that Congress at one time period. Some filled out unexpired terms and some were never sworn in.

Source: The Center for the American Woman and Politics, Eagleton Institute of Politics, Rutgers University.

Table 3

Summary of Women in the United States Congress
1917–1997

Congress	Term Years	Senate	House	Total Congress
65th	1917–1919	0 (0D, 0R)	1 (0D, 1R)	1 (0D, 1R)
66th	1919–1921	0 (0D, 0R)	0 (0D, 0R)	0 (0D, 0R)
67th	1921–1923	1 (1D, 0R)	3 (0D, 3R)	4 (1D, 3R)
68th	1923–1925	0 (0D, 0R)	1 (0D, 1R)	1 (0D, 1R)
69th	1925–1927	0 (0D, 0R)	3 (1D, 2R)	3 (1D, 2R)
70th	1927–1929	0 (0D, 0R)	5 (2D, 3R)	5 (2D, 3R)
71st	1929–1931	0 (0D, 0R)	9 (5D, 4R)	9 (5D, 4R)
72nd	1931–1933	0 (0D, 0R)	9 (5D, 4R)	9 (5D, 4R)
73rd	1933–1935	1 (1D, 0R)	7 (5D, 2R)	8 (6D, 2R)
74th	1935–1937	2 (2D, 0R)	6 (4D, 2R)	8 (6D, 2R)
75th	1937–1939	2 (1D, 1R)	6 (5D, 1R)	8 (6D, 2R)
76th	1939–1941	1 (1D, 0R)	8 (4D, 4R)	9 (5D, 4R)
77th	1941–1943	1 (1D, 0R)	9 (4D, 5R)	10 (5D, 5R)
78th	1943–1945	1 (1D, 0R)	8 (2D, 6R)	9 (3D, 6R)
79th	1945–1947	0 (0D, 0R)	11 (6D, 5R)	11 (6D, 5R)
80th	1947–1949	1 (0D, 1R)	7 (3D, 4R)	8 (3D, 5R)
81st	1949–1951	1 (0D, 1R)	9 (5D, 4R)	10 (5D, 5R)
82nd	1951–1953	1 (0D, 1R)	10 (4D, 6R)	11 (4D, 7R)
83rd	1953–1955	2 (0D, 2R)	11 (5D, 6R)	13 (5D, 8R)
84th	1955–1957	1 (0D, 1R)	16 (10D, 6R)	17 (10D, 7R)
85th	1957–1959	1 (0D, 1R)	15 (9D, 6R)	16 (9D, 7R)
86th	1959–1961	2 (1D, 1R)	17 (9D, 8R)	19 (10D, 9R)
87th	1961–1963	2 (1D, 1R)	18 (11D, 7R)	20 (12D, 8R)
88th	1963–1965	2 (1D, 1R)	12 (6D, 6R)	14 (7D, 7R)
89th	1965–1967	2 (1D, 1R)	11 (7D, 4R)	13 (8D, 5R)
90th	1967–1969	1 (0D, 1R)	11 (6D, 5R)	12 (6D, 6R)
91st	1969–1971	1 (0D, 1R)	10 (6D, 4R)	11 (6D, 5R)

(Table continues)

Table 3 (*continued*)

Summary of Women in the United States Congress
1917–1997

Congress	Term Years	Senate	House	Total Congress
92nd	1971-1973	2 (1D, 1R)	13 (10D, 3R)	15 (11D, 4R)
93rd	1973-1975	0 (0D, 0R0	16 (14D, 2R)	16 (14D, 2R)
94th	1975-1977	0 (0D, 0R)	19 (14D, 5R)	19 (14D, 5R)
95th	1977–1979	2 (2D, 0R)	18 (13D, 5R)	20 (15D, 5R)
96th	1979–1981	1 (0D, 1R)	16 (11D, 5R)	17 (11D, 6R)
97th	1981–1983	2 (0D, 2R)	21 (11D, 10R)	21 (11D, 10R)
98th	1983–1985	2 (0D, 2R)	22 (13D, 9R)	24 (13D, 11R)
99th	1985–1987	2 (0D, 2R)	23 (12D, 11R)	25 (12D, 13R)
100th	1987–1989	2 (1D, 1R)	23 (12D, 11R)	25 (13D, 12R)
101st	1989–1991	2 (1D, 1R)	29 (16D, 13R)	31 (17D, 14R)
102nd	1991–1993	4 (3D, 1R)	28 (19D, 9R)	32 (22D, 10R)
103rd	1993–1995	7 (5D, 2R)	47 (35D, 12R)	54 (40D, 14R)
104th	1995–1997	8 (5D, 3R)	47 (35D, 17R)	55 (35D, 20R)

Notes: Table shows maximum number of women elected or appointed to serve in that Congress at one time period. Some filled out unexpired terms and some were never sworn in.

Source: The Center for the American Woman and Politics, Eagleton Institute of Politics, Rutgers University.

In recent years the media have emphasized the "gender gap" in voting, suggesting that women as a group vote in greater numbers for Democratic candidates than for Republican candidates. In their research on voting patterns in the 1994 elections, Karlyn Bowman and Everett Carll Ladd found that the gender gap "has become a permanent feature of our politics," with women leaning toward Democrats and men toward the Republicans.[38] Bowman further concluded that since 1980, "men and women have voted differently in every national election."[39] According to Bowman, the "gender gap" is not a recent development, and it is likely to persist in the future.

Jody Newman of the National Women's Political Caucus has shown that the gender gap is only one of many differences in voting patterns. The gender gap is smaller than the partisan divide between Protestant and Jew, rich and poor, black and white, and rural and urban, for example.[40] That observation is in keeping with the historical record. Since the passage of the Nineteenth Amendment granting women the franchise, women have (despite predictions to the contrary) consistently remained divided on key issues. Factors like race, religion, education, and income all influence their vote.

Women have been voting at a steadily increasing rate for decades, finally matching the male voting rate in the 1980 elections. Since then, women have been voting in greater numbers than men, especially in national elections. Table 4 presents the small differences between the percentage of eligible men and women voting in presidential and nonpresidential elections. Notice, however, that because they account for a larger portion of adult Americans, equal percentages of eligible women voting translate into greater *numbers* of women than men voting in U.S. elections.

---

[38] Karlyn Bowman and Everett Carll Ladd, "Number Crunching: The 1994 Election Results, From *A* to *Z*," *Roll Call*, February 2, 1995.

[39] Karlyn Bowman, "The Gender Factor."

[40] Reported by Thomas Edsall, *Washington Post*, August 25, 1995, p. A10.

TABLE 4

Differences in Voter Turnout by Sex
1964–1994

Presidential Elections, 1964–1992

Election Year	% Voting Age Population Who Reported Voting		Number Who Reported Voting	
	Women	Men	Women	Men
1964	67.0	71.9	39.2 million	37.5 million
1968	66.0	69.8	41.0 million	38.0 million
1972	62.0	64.1	44.9 million	40.9 million
1976	58.8	59.6	45.6 million	41.1 million
1980	59.4	59.1	49.3 million	43.8 million
1984	60.8	59.0	54.5 million	47.4 million
1988	58.3	56.4	54.5 million	47.7 million
1992	62.3	60.2	60.6 million	53.3 million

Nonpresidential Elections, 1966–1994

Election Year	% Voting Age Population Who Reported Voting		Number Who Reported Voting	
	Women	Men	Women	Men
1966	53.0	58.2	31.8 million	30.7 million
1970	52.7	56.8	33.8 million	32.0 million
1974	43.4	46.2	32.5 million	30.7 million
1978	45.3	46.6	36.3 million	33.3 million
1982	48.4	48.7	42.3 million	38.0 million
1986	46.1	45.8	42.2 million	37.7 million
1990	45.4	44.6	43.3 million	38.7 million

Source: The Center for the American Woman and Politics, Eagleton Institute of Politics, Rutgers University.

Women, Poverty, and the Government

I f men were systematically advantaged in American society, one might expect to find many economic and social indicia in which men are persistently and steadily better off than women. There are many indicators by which men remain ahead of women, but the gap in most instances is shrinking, as described above.

Statistics paint an ambiguous portrait of the differences between men and women in the areas of health and crime. Men, for example, are far less susceptible than women to osteoporosis and gall bladder disease. Men are, however, statistically more likely than women to be victims of heart disease or the victims of murder, and women live longer than men, as is shown in figure 23. The

FIGURE 23
Life Expectancy at Birth by Sex
1920–1994

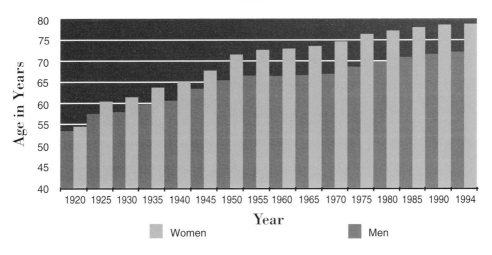

Note: 1994 data are preliminary.

Sources: *Historical Statistics*, vol. 1, Series B, pp. 107–115; *Statistical Abstract*, 1995, no. 114; *Vital Statistics*, 1985, no. 102; *World Almanac*, 1996, p. 974.

partial cause of some of those comparative statistics may well be a form of discrimination, a discrimination in the allocation of federal funds for research and development on diseases and funds for various forms of crime prevention. But it is difficult to determine whether the allocation of federal funds among thousands of competing programs works to the advantage or disadvantage of women.

■ Measures of Poverty

There is, however, one area where women consistently suffer more than men: poverty as measured by the federal government. Poverty disproportionately affects women in American society. Although women were 51.3 percent of the population in 1990, they accounted for 57.7 percent of all persons living in poverty. As figure 24 illustrates, between 1966 and 1994 female poverty rates consistently exceeded male rates by approximately three percentage points.[41] While absolute measures of poverty remain elusive and while government measures are often criticized, there is relatively little skepticism about the general finding of consistently greater incidence of poverty among women.

The statistics provide a number of clues about the life cycle of female poverty. For example, poverty rates for male and female children are almost equal. But between the ages of eighteen and twenty-four, women experience a 60 percent higher rate of poverty than men in the same age group. The rates differ significantly again among the elderly. The poverty rate among women over the age of sixty-five is twice the rate of men. Furthermore, the Department of Labor reports that between 1970 and 1990, female-headed households accounted for 99 percent of the increase in those living in poverty.[42] Demographic evidence suggests that this "feminization of poverty" will most likely continue.

Can government programs successfully target those female-headed households in poverty? Many federal programs already target predominantly female

---

[41] Data are not available before 1966.
[42] U.S. Department of Labor, *1993 Handbook on Women Workers*, pp. 37–38.

FIGURE 24
Percentage of Population below Poverty Line by Sex
1966–1994

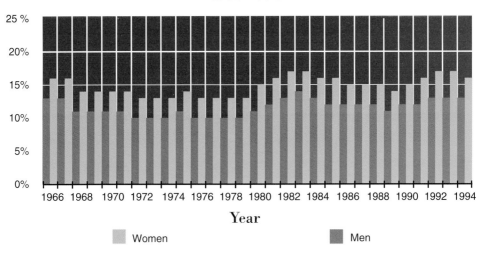

Source: U.S. Bureau of the Census, *Current Population Survey.*

single heads of households. Survivor benefits of government pension programs and Social Security primarily aid single, elderly women, and the Earned Income Tax Credit is intended to aid working unmarried heads of households.

Demographic trends also contribute to difficulties in tackling problems like female poverty. People are living longer, and women are living much longer than men, as is shown in figure 23. In 1920 male life expectancy was 53.6 years and female life expectancy was 54.6 years. By 1994 the life expectancy at birth for men had risen to 72.3 years and for women to 79 years. The differences in life expectancy between men and women in the United States do not reflect substantial differences in infant or child morbidity but rather significant differences in the death rates for middle-aged and elderly men and women. The net result is that there is a large and growing population of households consisting of single, elderly women. The proportion of the population that is elderly is growing, and the population that is elderly, single, and female is growing even more rapidly.

The federal definition of household *poverty*, a household with earned income below a specified target that varies with the number of household members, is an inaccurate gauge of economic well-being for households in all age groups. A family may have income below the poverty level but be eligible for a range of government programs that provide valuable but unmeasured benefits, for example, the earned income tax credit. A family or household below the poverty level may still have a satisfying level of consumption as a result of both its income and those government benefits. In contrast, a similar family with income slightly above the poverty rate may, by failing to qualify for certain government benefits, have a lower level of consumption than the family in "poverty."

Other factors also affect the interpretation of poverty. For example, a family of four earning $15,000 in rural Mississippi may have a substantially different form of poverty from that of a family of four earning $15,000 in midtown Manhattan. Government benefits for poor individuals and households vary substantially by demographic and health characteristics, from state to state, and even from locality to locality.

Households headed by elderly unmarried women are more likely than many other types of households to be in poverty for several reasons. The elderly, male and female, have few employment options to earn income. Most definitions of poverty measure only income, which is relatively easily to observe, rather than consumption or wealth, both of which are more difficult to observe. Yet the income patterns of an elderly household may have little relationship with either the consumption or wealth patterns of that household.

Poverty by any measure can still be acute for the elderly, particularly for female-headed households. Elderly households often consume savings built up over a lifetime. For elderly married couples, wives are more likely to survive their husbands by several years both because of a greater life expectancy and because women tend to marry men older than themselves. As a result, retirement savings, which may have been adequate at the date of retirement, may dwindle in later years when the wife is more likely to be a single survivor.

Young women are also heading up one-person households in unprecedented numbers, partly as a result of other demographic trends. Women are postponing marriage, thus creating a large population of young, single women. Between 1920 and 1970, as shown in figure 25, the median age of first marriage for women never exceeded 22 years of age. Since 1970, the median age of first marriage for women has steadily increased, reaching 24.5 years of age in the 1990s. That trend is largely the result of women's new educational and career opportunities. Now that significant numbers of women are attending college and pursuing professional lives upon graduation, they have delayed marriage and childbearing.

The rising incidence of divorce has also led to a much larger relative population of young single women. Figure 26 plots the increased incidence of divorce per 1,000 married women over the past few decades. Although divorce rates have plateaued since the mid-1970s, divorce is still much more common than in earlier decades. Figure 27 illustrates the distribution of American women age eighteen or older by marital status since 1950. In that year, 19.1 percent of adult women were single, and only 2.1 percent were divorced. By 1994, the percentage of single women grew only slightly to 19.7 percent, but the percentage of divorced women increased almost fivefold to 10.2 percent. Taken together, the postponed age of marriage and the high incidence of divorce have led to an increase in the relative population of young female-

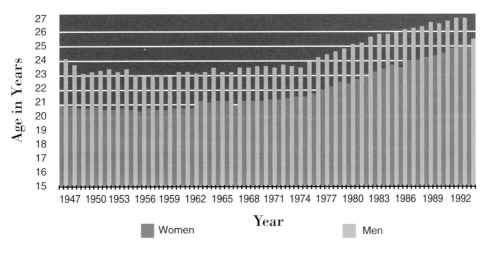

FIGURE 25

Median Age at First Marriage by Sex
1947–1994

Sources: U.S. Bureau of the Census, *Current Population Reports,* Series P, pp. 20–484.

FIGURE 26
Divorce Rates per 1,000 Married Women
1920–1994

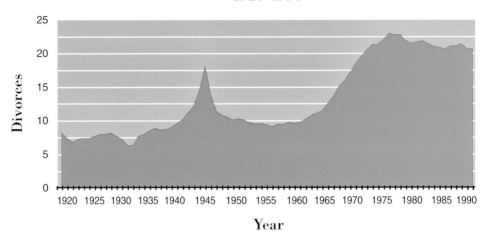

Note: 1991–1994 data are provisional.

Sources: *Historical Statistics,* vol. 1, Series B, pp. 216–220; *Vital Statistics:* 1971, pp. 2–6; *Statistical Abstract:* 1974. no. 93; 1978, no. 144; 1980, no. 124; 1982, no. 120; 1986, no. 124; 1991, no. 139; 1995, nos. 142 and 146; National Center for Health Statistics, unpublished data.

FIGURE 27
Marital Status of Women, Percentage Distribution
1950–1994

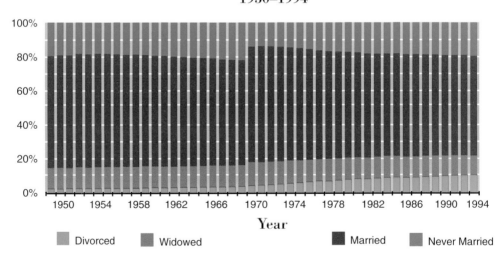

Note: Data for 1950–1970 include women 14 years old or older. Data since 1971 include women 18 years old or older.

Sources: *Statistical Abstract:* 1960, no. 36; 1962, no. 32; 1963, no. 31; 1964, no. 29; 1965. no. 29; 1966, no. 32; 1967, no. 32; 1969, no. 37; 1970, no. 36; 1971, no. 38; 1972, no. 46; 1980, no. 51; 1983, no. 44; 1989, no. 50; 1990, no. 50; 1991, no. 50; 1992, no. 49; 1993, no. 49, 1994, no. 59; 1995, no. 58. *Historical Statistics,* Series A, pp. 160–171.

headed households, a considerable percentage of which are vulnerable to poverty.

Many female-headed households have children present either from earlier marriages or from the increased rate of illegitimate births. As shown in figure 28, the illegitimacy rate in the United States increased from 7.1 illegitimate births per 1,000 unmarried women of childbearing age in 1940 to more than 45 illegitimate births per 1,000 unmarried women of childbearing age in 1994. At the same time, as shown in figure 29, the total birth rate was declining from 79.9 births per 1,000 women of childbearing age in 1940 to 68.9 births per 1,000 women of childbearing age in 1994. The net result is that the percentage of total American births that were illegitimate increased dramatically, while the proportion of families headed by unmarried women increased dramatically as well. Figure 30 shows that the percentage of families with children headed by women has more than tripled from 6.3 percent in 1950 to 22.5 percent in 1994.

FIGURE 28
Illegitimate Births per 1,000 Unmarried Women Ages 15-44
1940–1994

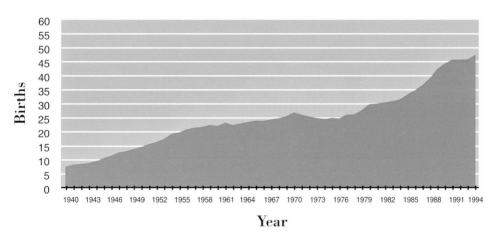

Sources: *Historical Statistics*, vol. 1, Series B, pp. 28–35; *Vital Statistics*: 1972, pp. 1–30, *Statistical Abstract*: 1980, no. 95; 1987, no. 86; 1990, no. 90; 1992, no. 89; 1994, no. 100; 1995, no. 94; and National Center for Health Statistics.

Even leaving aside the lower levels of social and educational achievement that often are associated with one-parent households, for several reasons families with children headed by an unmarried woman are more likely to live in poverty than is a family with two parents present. Family income for young families is based primarily on wage income rather than on income from accumulated capital. The opportunities for earned income are much greater with two earners than with one earner. More important, the choice of employment options is limited for the parent who bears most or all of the responsibility for child-rearing activities. The single parent is the only one who bears that responsibility and employment limitation. Those child-rearing activities consume time that could otherwise be spent earning income. Moreover, those activities make it difficult for a parent to accept employment with variable or uncertain hours, a characteristic of many jobs in the labor market. Unlike a one-parent family, the two-parent family can have both earners in the labor market, one of whom can accept a more highly compensated, variable-hour position.

FIGURE 29

Births per 1,000 Women Ages 15–44
1940–1994

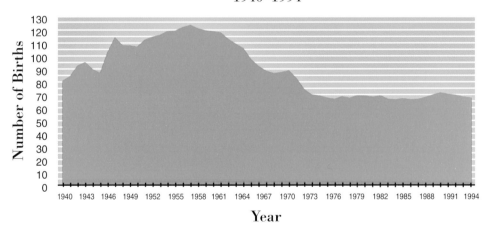

Sources: *Historical Statistics*, vol. 1, Series B, pp. 20–27; *Statistical Abstract*: 1979, no. 83; 1980, no. 87; 1982, no. 84; 1985, no. 82; 1994, no. 92; 1995, no. 93; and National Center for Health Statistics.

FIGURE 30

Percentage Distribution of Families with Children under 18
1950–1994

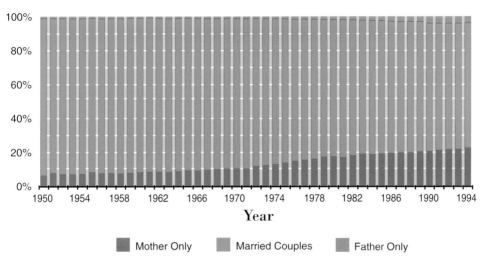

Source: U.S. Bureau of the Census, *Current Population Reports,* Series P, pp. 20–483, "Household and Family Characteristics: March 1994," and earlier reports.

■ Aid to Families with Dependent Children

Poverty-prone, unmarried, female-headed households are not entirely the result of independent demographic trends; some government programs themselves have influenced the great incidence of young female-headed households and the poverty associated with them. The federally funded Aid to Families with Dependent Children program (AFDC) provides entitlements to unmarried women—but not men—with children in poverty. The economically rational decision for a young, unmarried couple with a child but with few resources and few prospects for employment is to have the mother and the child, but not the father, apply for AFDC. By providing no equality of opportunity between the sexes for entitlements in poverty, AFDC helps ensure that there is no equality of outcome in the incidence of measured poverty. AFDC creates incentives for unmarried motherhood and disincentives for marriage and the enforcement of the parental responsibility of the father.

AFDC is a major source of income for unmarried mothers with children, and it influences decisions about the presence and the responsibility of the father. But AFDC is not the only program that may distort the observed poverty rate of households, particularly female-headed households. Once a household is in poverty, it is eligible for a number of benefits from federal and local governments. Those include such federally subsidized programs as Medicaid, food stamps, school lunch programs, and energy subsidies. Households are also eligible for locally sponsored programs such as day-care centers for children of high school students. Because many of those entitlement programs are open only to low-income households, many women who are heads of households correctly perceive that market employment would entail an enormous income loss, or what is essentially a "tax burden," due to the sacrifice of many of those entitlement benefits. Of course, if many of those entitlement programs were valued at market prices, many of those families might not be classified as being in "poverty."

Table 5 shows the estimated wage equivalent of welfare for a variety of states. Welfare income is defined as payments from AFDC, food stamps, Medicaid, public housing, and nutrition and utility assistance. The annual pre-tax wage equivalent of welfare for Hawaii, the most generous state, is $36,400. The least munificent state is Mississippi, with a figure of $11,500. The wage equivalent for the District of Columbia is $29,100.

Although poverty is an important economic indicator where women consistently trail men, it is far from obvious that discrimination in the marketplace is a substantial factor in the incidence of women in poverty or that government programs purporting to reduce sex discrimination in the market would have any noticeable effect on poverty rates. As is discussed below, discrimination in the employment offerings or in the payment of wages to women does not appear to be a central cause of poverty for most women. Indeed, women's poverty appears to be more the confluence of demographic trends and the unintended consequences of government programs.

TABLE 5

Estimated Wage Equivalent of Welfare by State
1995

Rank	Jurisdiction	Pretax Wage Equivalent ($)	Hourly Wage ($)	Rank	Jurisdiction	Pretax Wage Equivalent ($)	Hourly Wage ($)
1	Hawaii	36,400	17.50	27	Indiana	19,000	9.13
2	Alaska	32,200	15.48	28	Iowa	19,000	9.13
3	Massachusetts	30,500	14.66	29	New Mexico	18,600	8.94
4	Connecticut	29,600	14.23	30	Florida	18,200	8.75
5	District of Columbia	29,100	13.99	31	Idaho	18,000	8.65
6	New York	27,300	13.13	32	Oklahoma	17,700	8.51
7	New Jersey	26,500	12.74	33	Kansas	17,600	8.46
8	Rhode Island	26,100	12.55	34	North Dakota	17,600	8.46
9	California	24,100	11.59	35	Georgia	17,400	8.37
10	Virginia	23,100	11.11	36	Ohio	17,400	8.37
11	Maryland	22,800	10.96	37	South Dakota	17,300	8.32
12	New Hampshire	22,800	10.96	38	Louisiana	17,000	8.17
13	Maine	21,600	10.38	39	Kentucky	16,800	8.08
14	Delaware	21,500	10.34	40	North Carolina	16,800	8.08
15	Colorado	20,900	10.05	41	Montana	16,300	7.84
16	Vermont	20,900	10.05	42	South Carolina	16,200	7.79
17	Minnesota	20,800	10.00	43	Nebraska	15,900	7.64
18	Washington	20,700	9.95	44	Texas	15,200	7.31
19	Nevada	20,200	9.71	45	West Virginia	15,200	7.31
20	Utah	19,900	9.57	46	Missouri	14,900	7.16
21	Michigan	19,700	9.47	47	Arizona	14,100	6.78
22	Pennsylvania	19,700	9.47	48	Tennessee	13,700	6.59
23	Illinois	19,400	9.33	49	Arkansas	13,200	6.35
24	Wisconsin	19,400	9.33	50	Alabama	13,000	6.25
25	Oregon	19,200	9.23	51	Mississippi	11,500	5.53
26	Wyoming	19,100	9.18				

Note: Based on benefits available to a single mother with two children from the following programs: Aid to Families with Dependent Children (AFDC), food stamps, Medicaid, public housing, nutrition assistance, and utility assistance.

Source: Michael Tanner, Stephen Moore, and David Hartman, "The Work vs. Welfare Trade-off," *Cato Policy Analysis*, September 1995.

Evaluating Claims of Discrimination

It is impossible to untangle the many factors that have contributed to women's economic progress, since they include a strong economic structure that has created many new jobs, complex economic and demographic changes, political and social gains, and expanded personal choices. Legal barriers have fallen, too, enhancing women's opportunities for success. This monograph challenges the image of women as helpless victims in American society. The statistical evidence shows that American women have achieved startling gains since the early part of this century: the figures also suggest that they will continue to succeed.

A strong economy is the best antidote for possible discrimination. With a renewed demand for jobs, employers' profits fall if they turn away qualified candidates. The millions of jobs created in the 1980s drew women into the labor force and resulted in many of the advances we observe today. Most of the claims of discrimination against women are made either on grounds of employment discrimination or indirectly through claims of unusually high rates of poverty or other disadvantages for women. While individual instances of sex discrimination may occur, there is little evidence of systematic discrimination permeating the economy that would require considerable government intervention to eliminate.

Many remedies are available to combat discrimination. The Equal Pay Act states that women and men working for the same employer in the same establishment and under similar conditions must receive the same pay if their jobs require substantially equal skill, effort, and responsibility. Title VII of the Civil Rights Act of 1964 also prohibits wage discrimination based on sex and provides broader statutory protection of the right to equal pay. The Equal Employment Opportunity Commission is a bipartisan, five-member board charged with eliminating discrimination in employment practices, promoting equal opportunity programs, and investigating complaints of discrimination.

The original intent of many programs to end discrimination and provide equality of opportunity has been transformed into a new objective: equality of results. A set of new government programs, largely labeled under the heading of affirmative action, has debased the intent of the original laws that narrowly addressed equal opportunity. Where individual choices and market outcomes are not deemed to yield equality of results, affirmative action advocates propose remedies in the form of quotas, preferential treatment, and set-aside programs.

To be sure, supporters of affirmative action programs deny that they seek quotas or preferential treatment. Groups like the National Association of Women Business Owners claim that their goal is only "equal access." Yet as the above discussion of the "glass ceiling" and the "wage gap" suggests, assessing equal access is a complicated task that must involve a recognition that women often deliberately choose career flexibility or part-time work. The rallying cries of supporters of existing affirmative action programs rarely take such choices into account.

The new affirmative action programs have often looked at market outcomes uncritically. There is little conclusive evidence that women, with today's equal opportunity, face worse market outcomes purely or even partly as the result of sex discrimination. The standard of evidence necessary to demonstrate systematic market-wide sex discrimination against women is rarely if ever met.

■ Standards of Evidence

The battle for women's rights fought earlier this century focused on blatant discrimination written into statutes and regulations. It culminated in the passage of the Nineteenth Amendment in 1920, granting women the right to vote. Further reforms followed in the form of statutes and regulations that secured equal access for women in education, the professions, and equal status in the eyes of the law. The contemporary battle supposedly for women's "rights" by market skeptics is based not on *directly* observable defects of law but on *indirectly* observable differences in market outcomes that might result from discrimination against women. According to that perspective, equality of outcomes is the standard of evidence, not equality of opportunities.

While remedies exist for individual acts of sex discrimination, the challenge raised by the nonmarket advocates is that unequal outcomes are pervasive and economy-wide. The failure of markets to yield equal outcomes for women and men, they claim, reflects endemic discrimination. For example, more men become CEOs and more women become nurses, and average wages for women are still lower than those for men. The nonmarket advocates' preferred remedy is further federal government intervention that would provide not just for equal opportunity, but for equal outcome through such mechanisms as affirmative action and wages set not by markets but by federal agencies following "comparable-worth" criteria. Whether such pervasive discrimination exists is an inherently empirical question, but one that cannot be easily answered.

Unfortunately, the claims often rest on indirect rather than direct evidence. It is difficult to determine, for example, whether a woman's failure to reach the position of CEO is due to personal choice, market forces, or discrimination. The burden of proof should include the following analytical sequence: (1) statistical analysis of market data on the relative performance of men and women in a market; (2) the identification of plausible causes for any difference in the performance of men and women; and (3) a finding that some or all of the difference in the performance is plausibly the result of harmful discrimination against women.

In practice, however, the contemporary claims for government intervention to help women rarely follow that analytical path. The slightest anecdotal or descriptive evidence is proposed as conclusive of a disparity of market outcomes between men and women. "Women earn only seventy-two cents to the male dollar" is a favorite argument, but it is a statement devoid of context. Which group of women? In what profession? What other factors have been ignored to obtain that figure? Worse still, simple quantitative market information, such as wage rates, is sometimes packaged without analysis or interpretation as statistical evidence of a disparity between men and women. That masquerading of simple market information as conclusive evidence of the need for government interference for women is what this monograph seeks to challenge.

Data cited as evidence of systematic discrimination against women are often imprecise at best, and otherwise often misleading and unfounded. The irresponsible use of statistics can lead to harmful results. We live in a world where statistics are a part of our daily lives. They are used to define groups and, as importantly, to determine public policy. When used responsibly, statistics are a valuable map that can guide decision makers in their policy decisions. As existing statistics on women demonstrate, however, they can also be used irresponsibly by those who neglect important elements of social topography—personal choices and market forces, for example—in their assessment of the numbers.

There is, of course, an inescapable political dimension to statistical reasoning. Since the late nineteenth century, when the field of statistics took shape, people have complained bitterly of the biases of numbers. As the cliché suggests, "There are lies, there are damn lies, and there are statistics." Both the phrasing of questions in polling data and the classification of peoples in the census, for example, play an important role in determining the final figures. By far the most important element of statistical reasoning is interpretation. From row upon row of numbers, what questions will be asked? How nuanced an analysis will the translator perform?

Furthermore, even if plausibly harmful discrimination against women can be found in market data, government interference is not always the logical or successful remedy. Most statutory and regulatory discrimination against women has already been addressed in the legal realm; the easy changes have been made. Statutory changes are at best a blunt instrument to remedy alleged discrimination that results from unobservable social conditions. The results of the blunt instrument may well be imprecise, inefficient, and ineffective.

Conclusion

Since the earliest years of this century, American women have sought equal opportunities in education, the labor force, and the eyes of the law. This monograph has shown that in most of those areas women have achieved that equality. They are well represented in the professions, and they continue to enter fields of study that were previously dominated by men. Women are starting their own businesses in record numbers and winning elective offices throughout the country. Laws barring discrimination against women are on the books and enforced. All those gains clearly belie the image of women as victims struggling against discrimination in the workplace.

We have challenged the image of women as victims because it contradicts the obvious statistical gains American women have made in this century. It is also not an image with which most women identify. The countless women who have started their own businesses, won elective office, and made it to the top of their professions are not victims. They are evidence of just how far American women have come and how far they are going.

Many factors have contributed to that record of achievement. The reform efforts of suffragists in the nineteenth and early twentieth centuries were important, as were those of the feminists of the 1960s. American women owe a great deal to those who fought for the passage of civil rights legislation in the 1960s, particularly the Equal Pay Act of 1963 and the Civil Rights Act of 1964. Demographic and economic trends also shaped women's experiences.

The personal choices women have made are perhaps the most important and least appreciated factor in women's economic progress over the years. Decisions to enter previously male-dominated fields of education and employment, to marry and bear children later in life, to join the work force, and to leave the work force to raise children have all had an enormous effect on whether women can achieve total parity with men. Some of those choices, such as leaving the work force for a time to raise children, can have a negative effect on women's total lifetime earnings; others, such as entering previously all-male fields, have led to remarkable gains for women in the work force.

Unfortunately, that ambiguous legacy of choice is often ignored in favor of an image of women as victims of widespread discrimination. Such a portrayal of women overlooks an important factor: the possibility that many women do not want to reach the top of the corporate ladder. The mass media uncritically accepts as the standard of equality the requirement that women's achievements be statistically identical to men's achievements in all areas. That standard is insidious: it suggests that something is wrong if the highest salaries are not earned. That is insulting to all workers who choose flexibility, a friendly work-place environment, and other nonmonetary factors in the course of their careers.

Challenging those long-held assumptions about women is a perilous exer-cise, particularly because many groups have an investment in maintaining myths such as the wage gap and the glass ceiling. Both the wage gap and the glass ceiling are rhetorically useful but factually corrupt catch phrases. As we have demonstrated, those myths are harmful to women and do little to accu-rately describe the complex factors that determine a woman's place in the labor market. Important elements like education, consecutive years in the work force, and field of employment are not taken into consideration by those who generate pessimistic statistics about women's lack of progress. In addition, those who constantly point to the existence of a wage gap and a glass ceiling ignore one of the most important (but least statistically measurable) factors: personal choice.

The heterogeneity of the female population in this country guarantees that there will never be a consensus among women on all issues. From a statistical perspective, however, it is clear that women have made impressive gains: lev-els of education, wages, entrepreneurship, and employment have increased dramatically in the past several decades, and they will continue to improve. We have argued throughout this monograph that although women faced discrimi-nation in the past, that is only a small part of the story. The rest is a success story, and one that deserves to be told.

Bibliography

Abcarian, Robin. "Truth Is the Tool." *Enterprising Women* (July/August 1995): 20–21.

Becker, Gary S. *Human Capital: A Theoretical and Empirical Analysis, with Special Reference to Education.* New York: Columbia University Press (for National Bureau of Economic Research), 1964 2d ed., 1975.

Beller, Andrea H. "Occupational Segregation by Sex: Determinants and Changes." *Journal of Human Resources* (Summer 1992).

Bernstein, Nina. "Equal Opportunity Recedes for Most Female Lawyers." *New York Times* (January 8, 1996): A12.

Blau, Francine D. "Occupational Segregation and Labor Market Discrimination," in *Sex Segregation and the Workplace: Trends, Explanations, Remedies.* Edited by Barbara F. Reskin. Washington, D.C.: National Academy Press, 1984.

Blau, Francine D., and Andrea H. Beller. "Trends in Earnings Differentials by Gender, 1971–1981." *Industrial and Labor Relations Review* 41 (1988): 513–29.

Blau, Francine D., and Lawrence M. Kahn. "Race and Gender Pay Differentials," in *Research Frontiers in Industrial Relations and Human Resources.* Edited by David Lewin, Olivia S. Mitchell, and Peter D. Sherer. Madison, Wisc.: Industrial Relations Research Association, 1992.

Borger, Gloria. "What Do Women Want?" *US News and World Report* (August 14, 1995): 23–27.

Bowman, Karlyn. "The Gender Factor." *America at the Polls, 1994.* Storrs, Conn.: Roper Center for Public Opinion Research, 1995.

Bowman, Karlyn, and Everett Carll Ladd. "Number Crunching: The 1994 Election Results, From *A* to *Z*." *Roll Call* (February 2, 1995).

Brown, Clair, and Joseph Pechman. *Gender in the Workplace.* Washington, D.C.: Brookings Institution, 1987.

Cope, Sir Zachary. *The Early Diagnosis of the Acute Abdomen.* London: Oxford University Press, 1921, 14th ed., 1972.

Corcoran, Mary, and Greg J. Duncan. "Work History, Labor Force Attachment, and Earnings Differences between the Races and Sexes." *Journal of Human Resources* 14 (1979): 3–20.

Costello, Cynthia, and Barbara Kivimae Krimgold, eds. *The American Woman 1996–97.* New York: W. W. Norton & Company, 1996.

Davidson, Marilyn J., and Cary L. Cooper. *Shattering the Glass Ceiling.* United Kingdom: Paul Chapman, 1992.

De Witt, Karen. "Feminists Gather to Affirm the Relevancy of Their Movement." *New York Times* (February 3, 1996).

Dobrzynski, Judith. "Gaps and Barriers, and Women's Careers." *New York Times* (February 28, 1996): D2.

Edsall, Thomas. "Women's Political Caucus Plays Down Gender Gap." *Washington Post* (August 25, 1995): A10.

England, Paula. *Comparable Worth: Theories and Evidence.* Hawthorne, N.Y.: Aldine de Gruyter, 1992.

England, Paula, and George Farkas, Barbara Stanek Kilbourne, and Thomas Dou. "Explaining Occupational Sex Segregation and Wages: Findings from a Model with Fixed Effects." *American Sociological Review* 53 (1988): 544–58.

Even, William E., and David A. Macpherson. "The Decline of Private-Sector Unionism and the Gender Wage Gap." *Journal of Human Resources* 28 (1993): 279–96.

Federal Glass Ceiling Commission. *Good for Business: Making Full Use of the Nation's Human Capital.* Washington, D.C.: Government Printing Office, March 1995.

Fields, Judith, and Edward N. Wolff. "The Decline of Sex Segregation and the Wage Gap, 1970–80." *Journal of Human Resources* 26 (1991): 608–22.

Fillmore, Mary D. *Women MBAs: A Foot in the Door.* New York: G.K. Hall and Company, 1987.

Fitzpatrick, Kellyanne. "Beyond the Gender Gap." *Wall Street Journal* (May 17, 1996): A14.

Flanders, Stephen. "How Much Are Women Worth?" *Star Tribune* (October 2, 1995): 5A.

Fox-Genovese, Elizabeth. *Feminism Is Not the Story of My Life.* New York: Doubleday, 1996.

Gibbons, Robert, and Lawrence F. Katz. "Does Unmeasured Ability Explain Interindustry Wage Differentials?" *Review of Economic Studies* 59 (1992): 515–35.

Goldin, Claudia. "Career and Family: College Women Look to the Past." NBER Working Paper No. 5188; cited in the *National Bureau of Economic Research Digest* (December 1995).

Goldin, Claudia. "Life Cycle Labor Force Participation of Married Women: Historical Evidence and Implications." *Journal of Labor Economics* 7 (1989): 20–47.

Goldin, Claudia. *Understanding the Gender Gap.* New York: Oxford University Press, 1990.

Gramm, Wendy Lee. "Household Utility Maximization and the Working Wife." *American Economic Review* 65 (1975): 90–100.

Grimsley, Kirstin Downey. "From the Top: The Women's View." *Washington Post* (February 28, 1996): C1.

Groshen, Erica L. "The Structure of the Female/Male Wage Differential: Is It Who You Are, What You Do, or Where You Work?" *Journal of Human Resources* 26 (1991): 457–72.

Gupta, Nabanita Datta. "Probabilities of Job Choice and Employer Selection and Male-Female Occupational Differences." *American Economic Review Papers and Proceedings* 83 (1993): 57–61.

Hill, M. Anne, and June E. O'Neill. "Intercohort Change in Women's Labor Market Status." *Research in Labor Economics* 13. Edited by Ronald G. Ehrenberg. Greenwich, Conn.: JAI Press, 1992.

Himmelfarb, Gertrude. "A Sentimental Priesthood." *Times Literary Supplement* (November 11, 1994).

Holden, Karen C., and W. Lee Hansen. "Part-Time Work, Full-Time Work, and Occupational Segregation," in *Gender in the Workplace.* Edited by Clair Brown and Joseph A. Pechman. Washington, D.C.: Brookings Institution, 1987.

"Housework Gap." *Executive Female* (September 1989): 8.

"Housework Is Still Women's Work." *Numbers News* (April 1991): 3.

"Insight into the Glass Ceiling." *Enterprising Women* (July/August 1995): 13–14.

Johnson, George, and Gary Solon. "Estimates of the Direct Effects of Comparable Worth Policy." *American Economic Review* 76 (1986): 1117–25.

Jordan, Nick. "Labors Neither Loved Nor Lost: Changing Perceptions of Housework." *Psychology Today* 19 (October 1985): 70.

Killingsworth, Mark R. *The Economics of Comparable Worth.* Kalamazoo, Mich.: Upjohn Institute for Employment Research, 1990.

Kossoudji, Sherri A., and Laura J. Dresser. "Working Class Rosies: Women Industrial Workers during World War II." *Journal of Economic History* 52 (1992): 431–46.

Kosters, Marvin. "Wages and Demographics," in *Workers and Their Wages: Changing Patterns in the United States.* Edited by Marvin Kosters. Washington, D.C.: AEI Press, 1991.

Kristol, Irving. "Life without Father." *Wall Street Journal* (November 3, 1994).

Kristol, Irving. "Sex Trumps Gender." *Wall Street Journal* (March 6, 1996).

Larson, Elizabeth. "Victims in the Workplace?" *Investor's Daily* (June 4, 1995).

Leonard, Jonathan. "Women and Affirmative Action." *Journal of Economic Perspectives* 3 (1989): 61–75.

Lewenhak, Sheila. *The Revaluation of Women's Work.* United Kingdom: Earthscan, 1992.

McCormick, Katheryne, and Lytisha Williams. "Gender Gap a Factor in a Majority of Races in 1994." *News and Notes* (Center for the American Woman and Politics) (Winter 1994): 7–8.

Macpherson, David A., and Barry T. Hirsch. "Wages and Gender Composition: Why Do Women's Jobs

Pay Less?" *Journal of Labor Economics* 13 (1995): 426–71.

Marshall, Judi. *Women Managers Moving On.* New York: Routledge, 1995.

Mehta, Stephanie. "Number of Women-Owned Businesses Surged 43% in 5 Years through 1992." *Wall Street Journal* (January 29, 1996).

Mincer, Jacob. "Labor Force Participation of Married Women: A Study of Labor Supply," in *Aspects of Labor Economics.* Edited by C. Christ. Princeton: Princeton University Press, 1962.

Mincer, Jacob. "On-the-Job Training: Costs, Returns, and Some Implications." *Journal of Political Economy* 70, pt. 2 (October 1962): 50–79.

Mincer, Jacob. *Schooling, Experience, and Earnings.* New York: Columbia University Press (for the National Bureau of Economic Research), 1974.

Mincer, Jacob, and Haim Ofek. "Interrupted Work Careers: Depreciation and Restoration of Human Capital." *Journal of Human Resources* 17 (1982): 3–24.

Mincer, Jacob, and Solomon Polachek. "Family Investments in Human Capital: Earnings of Women." *Journal of Political Economy* 82 (March/April 1974): S76–S108.

Morrison, Ann M. *Breaking the Glass Ceiling: Can Women Reach the Top of America's Largest Corporations?* Reading, Mass.: Addison-Wesley, 1987.

Murphy, Kevin M., and Finis Welch. "The Role of International Trade in Wage Differentials," in *Workers and Their Wages: Changing Patterns in the United States.* Edited by Marvin Kosters. Washington, D.C.: AEI Press, 1991.

National Association of Women Business Owners. "Let's Stop the Affirmative Action Misinformation Campaign." Open letter to Pete Wilson. *PR Newswire* (June 8, 1995).

National Foundation for Women Business Owners. "Women-Owned Businesses Outpace All U.S. Firms." Press release. Washington, D.C.: Dun & Bradstreet Information Services, April 11, 1995.

Oaxaca, Ronald L., and Michael R. Ransom. "On Discrimination and the Decomposition of Wage Differentials." *Journal of Econometrics* 61 (1994): 5–21.

O'Neill, June. "The Causes and Significance of the Declining Gender Gap." Talk given at Bard College. September 22, 1994.

O'Neill, June. "Comparable Worth." *Fortune Encyclopedia of Economics.* Edited by David R. Henderson. New York: Warner Books, 1993.

O'Neill, June. "Comparable Worth: A Symposium on the Issues." Washington, D.C.: Equal Employment Advisory Council, 1982.

O'Neill, June. "The Determinants and Wage Effects of Occupational Segregation." Working paper. Washington, D.C.: Urban Institute, March 1983.

O'Neill, June. "Discrimination and Income Differences," in *Race and Gender in the American Economy.* Edited by Susan Feiner. Englewood Cliffs, N.J.: Prentice Hall, 1994.

O'Neill, June. "A Report on the Salaries of Economists." Study prepared for the American Economic Association, Commission on Graduate Education in Economics, January 1990.

O'Neill, June. "The Shrinking Pay Gap." *Wall Street Journal* (October 7, 1994).

O'Neill, June. "The Trend in the Male-Female Wage Gap in the United States." *Journal of Labor Economics* 3 (January 1985): S91–S116.

O'Neill, June. "Women and Wages." *The American Enterprise* (November/December 1990): 24–33.

O'Neill, June, and Solomon Polachek. "Why the Gender Gap in Wages Narrowed in the 1980s." *Journal of Labor Economics* 11 (1993): 205–29.

Pipes, Sally. "Glass Ceiling? So What?" *Chief Executive* (April 1996).

Pipes, Sally. "Through a Glass, Darkly." *Economist* (August 10, 1996).

Polachek, Solomon W. "Differences in Expected Post-School Investment as a Determinant of Market Wage Differentials." *International Economic Review* 16 (1975): 451–69.

Polachek, Solomon W. "Occupational Segregation among Women: Theory, Evidence and a Prognosis," in *Women in the Labor Market.* Edited by Cynthia B. Lloyd, Emily Andrews, and Curtis Gilroy. New York: Columbia University Press, 1979.

Polachek, Solomon W., and C. Kao. "Lifetime Labor Force Expectations in the Male-Female Earnings

Gap," in *New Approaches to the Analysis of Discrimination*. Edited by R. Cornwell and P. Wunnava. New York: Praeger, 1991.

Post, Katherine, and Michael Lynch. "Free Markets, Free Choices: Women in the Workforce." Briefing paper, Pacific Research Institute, December 11, 1995.

Post, Katherine, and Michael Lynch. "Smoke and Mirrors: Women and the Glass Ceiling." Pacific Research Institute Fact Sheet (November 1995).

"The Presidents and the Gender Gap." *The American Enterprise* (November/December 1991): 94–95. "Relatively Few Women Have Successful Careers and Family." *National Bureau of Economic Research Digest* (December 1995): 1.

Riggs, B. L., and L. J. Melton III. "The Prevention and Treatment of Osteoporosis." *New England Journal of Medicine* 327 (1992): 620–27.

Roper Starch Worldwide Survey. Cited in "Women and Work." *The American Enterprise* (March/April 1996): 91.

Smeal, Eleanor. Quoted in Kevin Merida. "Feminist Expo '96 Billed as Rebirth of the Women's Movement." *Washington Post* (February 4, 1996): A22.

Smith, James P. "Women's Wages and Work in the 20th Century." Santa Monica, Calif.: RAND Corporation, 1986.

Smith, James P., and Michael P. Ward. "Women in the Labor Market and in the Family." *Journal of Economic Perspectives* 3 (1989): 9–24.

Sommers, Christina Hoff. *Who Stole Feminism?* New York: Simon and Schuster, 1994.

Soreson, Elaine. *Comparable Worth: Is It a Worthy Policy?* Princeton: Princeton University Press, 1994.

Soreson, Elaine. *Exploring the Reasons behind the Narrowing Gender Gap in Earnings*. Washington, D.C.: Urban Institute, 1991.

Tanner, Michael, Stephen Moore, and David Hartman. "The Work *vs.* Welfare Trade-off." *Cato Policy Analysis* (September 1995).

U.S. Bureau of the Census. *Current Population Reports*. Series P-70, no. 10. Washington, D.C.: Government Printing Office, 1987.

U.S. Department of Labor. "Executive Summary." *Working Women Count: A Report to the Nation*. Washington, D.C.: Government Printing Office, 1994.

U.S. Department of Labor. *Facts on Working Women*. No. 95-1. Washington, D.C.: Government Printing Office, May 1995.

U.S. Department of Labor. *1993 Handbook on Women Workers*. Washington, D.C.: Government Printing Office, 1993.

"A Wealth of Working Women." *Economist* (June 8, 1996): 28.

"Women in the U.S. Congress 1996." Fact sheet. Rutgers, N.J.: Center for the American Woman and Politics, Eagleton Institute of Politics, Rutgers University, 1995.

Wood, Robert G., Mary E. Corcoran, and Paul N. Courant. "Pay Differences among the Highly Paid: The Male-Female Earnings Gap in Lawyers' Salaries." *Journal of Labor Economics* 11 (1993): 417–41.

William M. Landes
Clifton R. Musser Professor of
  Economics
University of Chicago Law School

Sam Peltzman
Sears Roebuck Professor of Economics
  and Financial Services
University of Chicago
  Graduate School of Business

Nelson W. Polsby
Professor of Political Science
University of California at Berkeley

George L. Priest
John M. Olin Professor of Law and
  Economics
Yale Law School

Murray L. Weidenbaum
Mallinckrodt Distinguished
  University Professor
Washington University

Research Staff

Leon Aron
Resident Scholar

Claude E. Barfield
Resident Scholar; Director, Science
  and Technology Policy Studies

Cynthia A. Beltz
Research Fellow

Walter Berns
Resident Scholar

Douglas J. Besharov
Resident Scholar

Robert H. Bork
John M. Olin Scholar in Legal Studies

Karlyn Bowman
Resident Fellow

Kenneth Brown
Visiting Fellow

John E. Calfee
Resident Scholar

Lynne V. Cheney
W. H. Brady, Jr., Distinguished Fellow

Stephen R. Conafay
Executive Fellow

Dinesh D'Souza
John M. Olin Research Fellow

Nicholas N. Eberstadt
Visiting Scholar

Mark Falcoff
Resident Scholar

John D. Fonte
Visiting Scholar

Gerald R. Ford
Distinguished Fellow

Murray F. Foss
Visiting Scholar

Diana Furchtgott-Roth
Assistant to the President and Resident
  Fellow

Suzanne Garment
Resident Scholar

Jeffrey Gedmin
Research Fellow

Robert A. Goldwin
Resident Scholar

Robert W. Hahn
Resident Scholar

Robert B. Helms
Resident Scholar; Director, Health
  Policy Studies

Glenn Hubbard
Visiting Scholar

Douglas Irwin
Henry Wendt Scholar in Political
  Economy

James D. Johnston
Resident Fellow

Jeane J. Kirkpatrick
Senior Fellow; Director, Foreign and
  Defense Policy Studies

Marvin H. Kosters
Resident Scholar; Director,
  Economic Policy Studies

Irving Kristol
John M. Olin Distinguished Fellow

Dana Lane
Director of Publications

Michael A. Ledeen
Resident Scholar

James Lilley
Resident Fellow; Director, Asian
  Studies Program

John H. Makin
Resident Scholar; Director, Fiscal
  Policy Studies

Allan H. Meltzer
Visiting Scholar

Joshua Muravchik
Resident Scholar

Charles Murray
Bradley Fellow

Michael Novak
George F. Jewett Scholar in Religion,
  Philosophy, and Public Policy;
  Director, Social and
  Political Studies

Norman J. Ornstein
Resident Scholar

Richard N. Perle
Resident Fellow

William Schneider
Resident Scholar

William Shew
Visiting Scholar

J. Gregory Sidak
F. K. Weyerhaeuser Fellow

Herbert Stein
Senior Fellow

Irwin M. Stelzer
Resident Scholar; Director, Regulatory
  Policy Studies

Daniel Troy
Associate Scholar

W. Allen Wallis
Resident Scholar

Ben J. Wattenberg
Senior Fellow

Carolyn L. Weaver
Resident Scholar; Director, Social
  Security and Pension Studies